If These
WALLS
Could **TALK:**
NEW YORK JETS

If These
WALLS
Could TALK:
NEW YORK JETS

Stories from the New York Jets
Sideline, Locker Room,
and Press Box

By Marty Lyons and Lou Sahadi

TRIUMPH
BOOKS

Library of Congress Cataloging-in-Publication Data
Names: Lyons, Marty, author. | Sahadi, Lou, author.
Title: If these walls could talk. New York Jets : stories from the New York
  Jets sideline, locker room, and press box / by Marty Lyons and Lou
  Sahadi.
Other titles: New York Jets
Description: Chicago : Triumph Books, 2020. | Summary: "This book is about
  the New York Jets football club"—Provided by publisher.
Identifiers: LCCN 2020018405 (print) | LCCN 2020018406 (ebook) | ISBN
  9781629377513 (paperback) | ISBN 9781641255325 (epub)
Subjects: LCSH: New York Jets (Football team)—History.
Classification: LCC GV956.N37 L86 2020 (print) | LCC GV956.N37 (eb-
ook) |
  DDC 796.332/64097471—dc23
LC record available at https://lccn.loc.gov/2020018405
LC ebook record available at https://lccn.loc.gov/2020018406

This book is available in quantity at special discounts for your group or organization. For further information, contact:
  Triumph Books LLC
  814 North Franklin Street
  Chicago, Illinois 60610
  (312) 337-0747
  www.triumphbooks.com

Printed in U.S.A.
ISBN: 978-1-62937-751-3
Design by Sadie Teper
Photos courtesy of Marty Lyons unless otherwise indicated

This book is dedicated to my family for always being there for me and my wife, Christine, for her love and support and her acceptance of who I am. My children, Rocky, Jesse, Megan, and Luke, continue to chase your dreams and thank you for all your support. My daughter-in-law, Lindsay, and my two grandchildren, Liv and Rush, thank you for making me smile.

—M.L.

CONTENTS

FOREWORD

I joined the New York Jets in 1977. I had already been there for two seasons when we had a big draft in 1979. That year Marty Lyons was the No. 1 draft choice out of Alabama, and Mark Gastineau was No. 2. The three of us, along with Abdul Salaam, would later become known as the New York Sack Exchange.

As soon as Marty arrived at the Jets, he started right away at defensive end. I was the defensive tackle, and Marty was playing next to me. Our union on the football field was the creation of what became a lifelong brotherhood.

During his rookie season, Marty was a sponge in terms of absorbing information, and I did my best to serve as a mentor to him. We were quickly becoming a really good team on that side of the line. The next year the team traded Lawrence Pillers to the San Francisco 49ers, and Mark was moved into a starting spot. I always felt badly for Lawrence. The poor guy got traded to the 49ers, and he was forced to suffer through winning multiple Super Bowls. Can you believe that?

Anyways, when Mark became the starting left end, I became the right end. Marty and Abdul became the interior linemen, and that made up the front wall of our 4-3 defense. The four of us became really close, and that led to a lot of success in those early years. When you are on a football team, you can't help but grow closer. If you are going to have success, you need to care for one another. That was the way Marty, Mark, Abdul, and I played together.

During that time Marty and I became almost inseparable. I remember telling Marty that he couldn't leave the weight room until I did because we had to play together for a long time, and he needed to be in there with me getting stronger every day. Marty took that to heart and he understood what it meant. One of my biggest attributes was always my strength. I was pretty much stronger than anyone I played against. Marty understood how important that was and he always worked hard in the weight room and on the football field, doing whatever it took to become a better player.

We certainly had our ups and downs as a team. Under head coach Walt Michaels, we played a postseason game against the Buffalo Bills in 1981, which was somewhere we had never been before. Obviously, that was very exciting. The next year the team was in a little bit of disarray after moving in a different direction from a coaching standpoint. During that time Marty and I took on the full responsibility of being the leaders of our defense. Marty was more of a vocal leader than I was, and I guess you can say that I was more a of lead-by-example kind of guy. Marty has always been a very emotional person, as he still is today as the leader of his foundation. Back then most of the tables in the locker room had been broken by Marty during the pregame.

Back in 1981 I shot up my foot for 11 or 12 games. The reason why I had to get my foot shot up? Because Marty stepped on it! I'm not joking when I say that I got hurt more often by Marty than I did by anyone I ever played against. But I also ended up becoming Defensive Player of the Year that same season, so maybe I should thank Marty for stepping on my foot that day. In a funny way, it ended up being one of those things that brought us even closer together.

As the years went on, we ended up having success in the mid-1980s, and it all started with the defensive line, and the play of Mark was so instrumental in that success. Abdul had been traded to the San Diego Chargers around that time.

Closer to the end of my career, I suffered a really bad knee injury and didn't play much that year. It was getting to a point at that time where everyone knew the head coach and I weren't getting along. I told my friend, "Marty, you know there is not a whole lot of people who are standing beside me right now." And then he told me, "Kleck, your ship is sinking. I'm not going down with it!" That was his way of bringing humor into a tough situation. Marty was always a great friend and he was always there for me.

After we were done playing, fans still wanted to see the New York Sack Exchange. Marty, Mark, Abdul, and I would go out and do a lot of appearances and speaking engagements together. Marty and I became pretty good public speakers and we often found ourselves together at various events. During that time we also started to understand what it meant to have a family inside of our family. Marty was growing his family outwardly with his foundation and he became an extroverted person who considered everyone who got involved with it to be a part of his family.

For example, John Nitti was a guy who played running back with us for a few seasons. He eventually became a part of Marty's foundation, and that made him a part of Marty's family. Marty started the foundation with Kenny Schroy, who played strong safety for us, was a very good football player, and is now family to Marty for the rest of his life. I can name numerous other people who have that same type of relationship with Marty, and he considers them all to be a member of his family.

Family is something that has always been very important to Marty and me, which I think is one of the main reasons that we have always been so close. My wife and children are very important to my life, as it should be, and Marty always had those same values as well.

I also believe that the Lord steps into your life during times of both good and bad. I think Marty understood that sentiment when he created his foundation. Over a six-day span in 1982, a young boy he mentored as a Big Brother passed away, he lost his father, and his first son, Rocky, was born. That's what inspired him to establish his foundation, and it really instilled that family aspect into his life. Family values are something that brought Marty and I even closer together when we were done playing.

Knowing how dedicated Marty is, it came as no surprise to me that his foundation quickly took on a life of its own. It quickly grew into something that has been a blessing for so many people. Marty may have never believed that it would become so impactful in the beginning, but it is his sense of family that makes so many people want to be a part of what he is doing. His brothers are even running two different chapters for him in two different states.

Marty and I went to meet with a young lady in Maryland who called him about her son. She had a special needs child who needed oxygen and a bed for their home. When Marty visited them, he found out that not only did she have the one child with special needs, but she also had two children who needed some assistance. She was just too humble to ask for help beyond the first child. Without any hesitation Marty decided to take care of both children. He wanted to do whatever he could to help their family live a better life.

Although Marty may be a big, imposing guy who played football, he is someone who always wears his heart on his sleeve. When he speaks about a child or family that his foundation is supporting, he becomes very emotional. He is so wrapped up into every single person who has been granted a wish through his foundation. I don't want to put him on the spot, but I bet he can still tell you the name of every kid he has helped over the years.

Marty makes so many people happy. The joy he spreads is something that I am not sure he will truly understand until he passes to the other side. Marty has always been seen as this larger-than-life human being. If you ask Marty, he would never want to be recognized as that. He always wants the spotlight shining on someone else. He has done so many good deeds for so many people and he has accomplished so much both on and off the football field.

When the day comes that Marty crosses to the other side and stands in front of the Lord, he will be patiently waiting for words to come out of our Lord's mouth. And I believe that the words he will hear from our Lord will be: "Well done, my good and faithful servant."

—Joe Klecko
New York Jets defensive lineman 1977–87

INTRODUCTION

I asked myself why at the age of 62 would I want to write a book about the New York Jets? Well, for the last 40 years, the Jets have been a big part of my life. From a player, to a TV host, to now being a part of their radio team for 18 years, I owe the Jets a lot. Sometimes we measure the greatest of an organization by how many Super Bowl trophies it has. Many times we forget about the people inside the organization who dedicated their lives to the game of football and the players they coached. From my first day there in 1979, the Jets organization supported me and it continues to support me and my foundation today. They don't have to do it. Hell, football is a business, and I got paid as a player, but the Jets chose to support me because they believed in me as a person. My motivation in writing is not only to give you insight into my opinion of players and coaches who have crossed my path in the last 40 years, but also for the incredible kids who were cheated out of life by being born with cancer. I want to pay tribute to their lives. When I started the Marty Lyons Foundation in 1982, I never knew that 37 years later it would grow to what it is today. Although many have left us way too soon, their memories will live on.

The proceeds for the sale of this book will go directly to the foundation to help provide a special wish to a special child diagnosed with a terminal illness.

Fifty years ago we were able to put men on the moon, and 50 years later, we are searching for a cure for cancer. Cancer will affect everyone in our lifetime. My hope is to bring a new awareness to childhood cancer so that we can make tomorrow better for a lot of their families and one day beat it.

—Marty Lyons

INTRODUCTION

I was a magazine editor in New York when the eight-team American Football League was formed, and within 48 hours, the doubters dubbed it "The Foolish Club." The conjecture was they would never be successful challenging the rock solid NFL. I wasn't of that belief. The AFL was indeed a big underdog, but with television fueling the AFL, I believed it had a chance with NBC, another TV sponsor. I thought it had such a chance that I was the first magazine editor to feature an AFL player on the cover.

That was the beginning of my close relationship with the burgeoning New York Jets. Years later I traveled with the team on a number of road games. By the late 1960s, I developed a trusting relationship with quarterback Joe Namath. When the Jets upset the heavily favored Baltimore Colts in Super Bowl III, I became an author. World Press contracted me to write *The Long Pass*—the first of my 27 books.

My relationship with the Jets continued into the 1979 season, where I established a close relationship with Marty Lyons, and it has remained close to this day. There aren't enough plaudits to bestow on Marty—not only as a player, but also as a caring and giving person. The Marty Lyons Foundation, which grants wishes for terminally ill children, is perhaps his greatest gift.

From his visit to my Palisades, New York, home with Alabama teammates—running back Tony Nathan and linebacker Barry Krauss—to his appearance at my surprise 50th birthday party when he brought safety Kenny Schroy and a personalized Jets jersey emblazoned with No. 50, I have so many good memories of our friendship. That jersey remains the centerpiece of my memorabilia room in Boca Raton to this day.

When Marty asked me to assist with his long overdue, anecdote-filled book, I didn't hesitate. How could I? Marty is my Hall of Famer.

—*Lou Sahadi*

CHAPTER 1
1960: The Birth of the Jets

He was shy, wore glasses, and had the outward appearance of a choirboy. Lamar Hunt was only 26 years old, but he had guts and he had money. Barely four years out of college, Hunt wanted to own a professional football team in 1959.

At the time Hunt was in the oil business in Dallas with a company owned by his father, H.L. Hunt. He was a frustrated football player at Southern Methodist University where he sat on the bench for his entire three-year career. In fact, he sat so far down on the bench that no one knew him. "I had received two letters at SMU," recalled Hunt somewhat sheepishly. "The first letter came from coach Marty Bell at the end of my senior year. It read: 'Dear Lamar: please stay off our football field. You have cluttered it up long enough.' The second letter I got was also from Marty Bell: 'Dear Lamar: please return to the athletic department the 12 T-shirts you've taken the past three years.'"

Imagine someone like Hunt trying to buy a professional football team? He zeroed in on Chicago, a two-team city at the time, where George Halas and his Bears owned Chicago while the Cardinals, who were owned by the Wolfner family, were floundering. It was Hunt's intention to purchase the Cardinals and move them to Dallas. "I remembered some of the people the Cardinals mentioned," Hunt said. "Bud Adams stood out in my mind. Then there were people in Minnesota and Seattle, and it went on from there. It was up to me to go out and recruit the owners."

In January of 1959, Hunt went to Houston to meet Adams, another wealthy Texan who owned Ada Oil Company as well as being a rancher, investor, cattle breeder, and a real estate developer. Hunt and Adams were complete opposites. Hunt was quiet, unassuming, dressed conservatively, and appeared reserved. He could have easily been mistaken for a librarian.

On the other hand, Adams was what a typical Texan was supposed to be: flamboyant in his 10-gallon hat, cowboy boots, and on occasion a startlingly white leather coat. Hunt and Adams were the two pivotal persons who launched the American Football League the following year.

Hunt spearheaded the movement with a modest gameplan of recruiting other owners in six cities. He got a yes from Bob Howsam in Denver and received the pledges of Max Winter, E. William Boyer, and H. P. Skoglund in Minnesota. With four cities verbally committed, Hunt looked toward New York and found a willing owner in nationally known sportscaster Harry Wismer. The sixth city on Hunt's list was Los Angeles, and he succeeded in getting a nod from hotel scion Baron Hilton.

By July Hunt had six lined up for the league's inaugural season in 1960.

Hunt felt it was time to meet with NFL commissioner Bert Bell. Davey O'Brien, who worked for Lamar's father, set up the meeting.

Bell appeared receptive. He felt that the new league would succeed and assured Hunt that the NFL would not do anything to harm its chances. "I'm all for the new league and would help nurture it," Bell said. "The more teams and the more competition, the better."

Despite Bell's statements the owners in the NFL were privately against any new leagues. However, the owners felt that any new league would not survive. The disbanding of the All-American Conference just 10 years before was still fresh in their minds.

On the suggestion of Wismer, the ever publicity conscious Titans owner, Hunt and Adams agreed to hold the first meeting of the league on August 14 in Chicago at the Hilton Hotel. Wismer suggested the date because that was the weekend of the College All-Star Game, and writers from all over the nation would be in Chicago covering the game between the collegians and the champions of pro football.

At the meeting six cities were represented by eight individuals: Hunt (Dallas); Adams (Houston); Wismer (New York); Howsam (Denver); Hilton (Los Angeles); and Winter, Boyer, and Skoglund (Minneapolis).

They announced the league would begin play in 1960 and that they would hold another organization meeting in Dallas on August 22. On that day each owner agreed to provide a $100,000 performance bond and place $25,000 in cash into the league's account and adopted the name American Football League.

On October 28 in Wismer's New York apartment, Hunt met with Ralph Wilson, who owned an insurance company and a trucking firm in Detroit. Wilson committed to a franchise in Buffalo. The fledgling league now had seven members. The final piece of the puzzle was Boston, where Billy Sullivan was raising money through a unique public stock offer.

Sullivan was fully prepared to make his presentation at the November meeting in Minneapolis. Everything appeared to be going smoothly. Sullivan would be formally accepted as the league's eighth member.

At the next day's meeting, Sullivan was in shock. He had a pocketful of money and was ready to celebrate being accepted as the AFL's eighth and final member when his Minneapolis hosts betrayed him. However, the Minneapolis group convinced the owners that they were still committed to the AFL and were allowed to participate in the draft.

The owners also adopted a cooperative television plan whereby the league office would negotiate the television contract, the proceeds of which would be divided equally among the member teams. It was a plan that was later adopted by the NFL.

A week later the owners named Joe Foss, a former World War II flying hero and former two-term governor of South Dakota, commissioner for a three-year term. A ruggedly handsome 44-year-old, Foss was a recipient of the Congressional Medal of Honor and was folksy as Mark Twain. It was said he couldn't have been more honest if he tried.

On June 9 Wismer, who was head of the league's television committee, gave the AFL instant credibility. He finalized a five-year deal with ABC. The first year's revenue would amount to $1,785,000 with graduated increases for each of the remaining four years. It was the first financially rewarding deal the new league made.

With a television contract and a favorable court decision, the AFL was primed for its inaugural season that was less than three months away.

Wismer attempted to occupy the deserted Polo Grounds, which had been empty since the baseball Giants' exodus to San Francisco in 1958, by adding touches of glamour. He made an offer to the Giants' popular defensive end, Andy Robustelli, to become coach of the Titans. But instead Robustelli used the offer as leverage to receive another year's contract from the Giants. Wismer then turned to the legendary Sammy Baugh as his coach. The first player that Wismer signed was a future Hall of Famer: Don Maynard, who had played two years for the Giants before playing a year in the Canadian League.

As expected, no team turned a profit that first season. Total league losses were estimated to be between $2 million and $3 million. Total attendance was registered at 92,236 with a per game average of 16,558. Citing increased sports competition in Los Angeles, Hilton moved the Chargers to San Diego for the 1961 season.

Unfortunately, the worst draw was the Titans. It taxed Wismer financially and hurt the league's image. The team's office, though it had a Park Avenue address, was Wismer's apartment. The entrance to the building was on 49th Street. Pity the poor ticket buyer who was looking for the Titans' office on Park Avenue.

Wismer used the living room for his office while the coaches used the dining room. A small foyer served as the ticket department. The publicity man's office was the butler's pantry while the bathroom served as the mimeograph room where the releases were turned out. It was the only office like it in the AFL.

The press scoffed at the relatively low attendance numbers released by Wismer. George Vecsey of *The New York Times* wrote, "The fans came disguised as empty seats." The empty stands were not lost upon the players either. They actually made light of it. Erudite Titans linebacker Larry Grantham was one. "There were so few fans at the games that we used to wave to our wives in the stand," Grantham quipped. "During the game we'd hear the announcement that there were 19,000 or 20,000 people. We knew there were only 2,000 or 3,000 in the park. I used to tell a story at some dinners that the Titans didn't line up on the field for the pregame introductions. We went into the stands and shook hands with everyone."

The 1961 season wasn't much better. All that New York, the league's flagship city, could offer was the antiquated Polo Grounds, which was such an eyesore that it caused the Giants to leave for Yankee Stadium six years earlier. Wismer's dollar losses were mounting. Fans were not breaking down the door to his Park Avenue apartment to purchase season tickets.

The first crisis came the third week of the season when the players' paychecks bounced. The players refused to practice all week. Finally, on their own, they worked out Friday, went to Buffalo on Saturday, and defeated the Bills 17–6. In the dressing room before the game, someone shouted, "Let's go out and win one for the Gipper."

Finally, in the first week in November, Wismer gave up. He turned to his enemy, Foss, and admitted that he was broke. Foss was ready with a willing buyer in Sonny Werblin, the head of Music Corporation of America.

Werblin began with a new name. Less than a month after he purchased the Titans, Werblin announced that the new name of the team would be the Jets. At the same time, he introduced Weeb Ewbank, who two months before had been released as head coach of the Baltimore Colts, as the new coach and general manager. Ewbank was well known in professional football. He had won two championships for the Colts after having taken over in a similar situation to the Jets—namely, a vast rebuilding job.

Werblin's dynamism was apparent in the Jets' first season in Shea Stadium in 1964. Matt Snell, a running back out of Ohio State, was the Jets' No. 1 draft choice. He was also drafted by the Giants, but the "Werblin Way" caused Snell to sign with the Jets. Snell finished as Rookie of the Year, and it paid off at the ticket office. Although the Jets went 5–8–1, they drew record crowds in their new home, averaging 45,000 a game. The success of the Jets in their first season at Shea Stadium made it obvious that the AFL was permanently established in New York.

Snell's signing signaled two important events. It indicated that the AFL was now willing to pay whatever price necessary to obtain college stars. Even more importantly, the acquisition of Snell was a severe blow to the prestige of the Giants. They could no longer ignore the AFL team.

Werblin wasn't through. At the end of the 1964 season, he took a giant step toward building a winner by going after Alabama quarterback Joe Namath, the nation's top-rated passer. Alabama coach Paul W. Bryant called Namath "the greatest athlete I have ever coached." He was the prize of the draft, and Werblin was determined to sign him. It would be a major coup for the AFL. He did so by beating out the Giants again with a staggering $427,000 contract that left the NFL breathless.

Werblin saw other things in Namath beyond the playing field. He saw a handsome, dark-haired youngster who generated sex appeal. He was an instant box office star, an athletic hero, and Hollywood star all rolled into one. There was no question in Werblin's mind that Namath was the one.

With the owners finally coming to the painful realization that they were losing the game to the players, the leagues grudgingly agreed to merge. Gone now were the big bonuses, the baby-sitting, and the cloak and dagger intrigue for players.

The merger didn't sit well with Oakland Raiders owner Al Davis, who was named the AFL's commissioner less than three months before. He had the NFL on the run by getting a number of its stars to sign up

My wife, Christine, and I stand next to Joe Namath, one of the legends of the AFL days.

for the younger league. The merger also was costly to the AFL because it was required to pay an $18 million indemnity to the NFL over a 20-year period.

Werblin was upset and perhaps justifiably so. Along with Davis, he had been a hawk who led the fight. After coming out on top, his wings were now clipped. "I am disgusted, completely disgusted with the way things went," he told a close associate. "How can I not sell the Jets, considering the way things are going? We had the whole thing won and now we are giving it back."

Two years later, a disillusioned Werblin walked away. He sold out his interests in the Jets, a team he had pulled from the ashes to the talk of pro football. Two years later with Namath as their quarterback, the Jets upset the mighty Colts in Super Bowl III. Every underdog in America now related to the Jets.

It was the AFL's only victory in the three Super Bowl games played. It was the crowning achievement of a league that came in from the cold against all odds.

CHAPTER 2
From Florida to Alabama

Growing up in Pinellas Park, Florida, from a family of seven kids in 1960 wasn't easy. My parents believed in three things: family, sports, and education. Being a registered nurse, my mom, Thelma, was the breadwinner of the family, and my father was a retired cop on disability. All seven of us went to the same high school, and after my first two older brothers, Jim and Richard, graduated, a shadow over the Lyons name had been cast. If you were a Lyons, expectations had been set, and standards were high.

My father, Leo, believed in discipline—old-style discipline, hands-on discipline. Yes sir, no sir wasn't an option. It was expected, and he demanded it. My father was old school. He gave you one chance to correct yourself. If you answered a question with "okay" or any other response, he would land a back hand on your chest or sometimes around the chin area. He believed that there would come a time in your life where you would be a reflection of the values your parents taught you. Looking back on it some 50 years later, I still respect my dad, but it wasn't going to be the way I would raise my four children. And it wasn't.

My father was also my first baseball coach in Little League. Hard work, discipline, and hustle was his way of playing.

My mother, Thelma, was a saint. When she wasn't working, she was at the ball field supporting us the best she could. I remember going with her when I was in sixth grade to watch my brother, Richard, play in a basketball game. Richard was good. I told myself that I wanted to be that good, and if I could be better than him, I would be something special. My oldest brother, Jim, was a swimmer and an outstanding student. Later in high school when I needed to get away from the recruiting merry-go-round, Jim and his wife, Sharon, were always there.

My brother, Richard, was really the hero that I looked up to. He matched his outstanding basketball skills with his performance in the classroom. After Richard graduated from high school, he accepted an appointment to attend West Point and made a career in the Army. My

I stand in front of the house in Takoma Park, Maryland, where my other six siblings and I were born.

older sister, Jackie, was an outstanding softball player and volleyball player. She was tougher than nails and probably kicked my ass until I was a sophomore or junior in high school. My younger sister, Theresa, was an honor student, and my younger brother, Phil, was a student-athlete with big shoes to fill since he was the fifth boy out of the Lyons' family at the same high school. But it was brother, Dan, that showed me the ways both on and off the field. Theresa and Phil were athletic, but they were better in the classroom than they were on the playing field.

Dan was two years older than I and meaner than a snake. He was a three-sport athlete in football, basketball, and track. Dan taught my first lesson in life: never quit on yourself.

It was a hot summer day in Florida as we were going through two-a-days practices at St. Pete Catholic/Bishop Barry. The head coach, Bill Klier, was running a drill called the hamburger drill. It was a simple drill where the quarterback would hand the running back the ball, and I would have to run over the tackler between two dummies. Coach Klier was your typical high school head football coach of the early 1970s with Bike coaching shorts, T-shirt, whistle around his neck, high white socks (one higher than the other), baseball mesh hat, and, of course, a clipboard used for hitting players on their helmets more so than holding notes. As a freshman I was a running back. The drill started one day when Coach Klier grabbed me by my facemask and told me, "There is no one out here that can tackle you."

Oh, by the way, Coach Klier was a spitter. The first time I ran the ball, I got killed. All I could hear was Coach Klier yelling, "run it" again. This happened over and over again until the sixth time of running the ball. That's when I got lucky and ran the tackler over. Coach Klier grabbed my facemask once again and said, "Remember that, son. No one can tackle you."

Well, the next morning, when my brother, Dan, came to wake me up for practice, I told him that I was quitting. I said Coach Klier was nuts, and he was a wild man. I continued to yell that I didn't need him or football anymore. Dan pulled me out of my bed and said, "If you quit now, you'll continue to quit the rest of your life." I learned right there at that moment that he was right. Quitting shouldn't be an option if you want to be the best.

The other value lesson I learned in high school was learned the hard way. It was at baseball practice my freshman year. It was a JV squad game with the varsity team. I was a pitcher, threw to a few batters, and then went to sit on an old duffel bags of bats. The next batter hit a fly ball to the left fielder. As he got ready to catch the ball, the afternoon sun got into his eyes, and the ball hit him right in the forehead. Everyone started laughing, but by the time I looked up, the varsity coach was running straight at me. He hit my face with his forearm. As I was falling backward, he grabbed me by my shirt, pulled me up off the ground, popped me a couple of more times, yelling "Who the hell do you think you are, laughing at one of your teammates?" I learned from that day forward to never put yourself above anyone. It's one of those lessons that has stayed with me.

George O'Brien, my last high school head football coach, had the most influence in my life in high school. He saw more in me than I saw in myself. When I was a sophomore, he started sending out letters to different colleges, saying that I could play. By my senior year, letters and invites were coming in the mail on a weekly basis from places like Alabama, Tennessee, Florida, Florida State, Kentucky, and Miami. They were sending scouts to every Friday night game. St Pete Catholic was a small private school, and we probably only had 26 to 28 players on the football team. If you were good enough to play offense, then you were good enough to play defense and special teams. I played fullback, linebacker, punter, and sometimes even kicked off. Offers for a football scholarship were on my table, and I talked to Coach O'Brien after every visit. I would ask him where I should go, and he always had the same response, "You make your decision, and I'll tell you if you were right."

When I chose Alabama, Coach Bryant personally came to my house to sign me. It was a thrill for my entire family. To come home from a basketball game and see Coach Bryant sitting there with my father, having a beer, and holding a scholarship letter for me to sign, what a sight that was. Coach O'Brien confirmed afterward that Alabama was the right choice for me. Coach Bryant never made me any promises. He just said, "If you're good enough to play, the opportunity will be there for you."

I owe thanks to my high school teammates, especially Ted LaVenture, Tim Ginty, Joe Ezzo, and friends like Ron Nuzzo, Rob Smith, Mary Kippen, and Kathy Zawada for all of their support.

When I graduated from St. Pete Catholic in 1975, I was considered a big fish in a small pond. I was All-State in three sports: football, basketball, and baseball. When I got to Alabama in the summer of '75, that resume didn't matter. Alabama had the best of the best. Hell, the guy next to me was All-State in three sports, and the guy next to him was All-State in four sports. I was now the small fish in a great ocean of talent from around the country.

My mom, Dan, and Phil made the drive from Pinellas Park, Florida to Tuscaloosa, Alabama, which took us about 11 hours. The next day, before I had to report to the athletic field, my mom thought it would be a good idea to open a bank account for me. We went to The First Bank of Alabama and met Jimmy Mills, who was your typical southern gentleman: soft spoken and polite. When he asked my mom how much she would like to open the account with, she politely said, "$100, I think that should last him the year." Yep, bless her heart, $100 was a lot for my parents to give up, and I was grateful. Between that and the $15 a month the athletic department gave us for doing our laundry, I was in fat city.

As a freshman the first person I met was Willie Meadows, the equipment manager. He always seemed to be mad. I told him who I was, and he slid a netted bag to me and said, "Here's your jock, socks, shorts, and T-shirt. If you want it washed after practice, throw it in the basket after practice with it pinned together, and we'll clean it. Don't lose them. They won't be replaced." I looked down at the oversize safety pin, and it had the No. 93 on it. That's how I found out what my college number would be. I still have that No. 93 safety pin in my trophy cabinet at home.

Practices were hell. Coach Bryant believed in hard work. Every practice had this theme of "gut check" to it. Coach Bryant wanted to know which players he could count on and trust. His philosophy was simple. He would rather have a player quit on himself or his team in practice rather than in a game where it really counted. Coach Bryant and his staff had their priorities for the team in place: always be proud of your family, always be proud of your faith, get your education, and win some football games. That's exactly what we did. That class of '75 went 42–6, won three SEC titles, and won a national championship. We were loaded with talent with guys like Jeff Rutledge, Tony Nathan, Barry Krauss, Murray Legg, Rich Wingo, and David Hannah.

We opened the '75 season with an embarrassing 20–7 loss to Missouri. When we got back to practice the next day, there was a reminder. In the middle of the turf field under Coach Bryant's tower, "20–7" was painted. To this day no one has claimed that they painted that message. Rumor had it that it was someone on Coach Bryant's staff who was sending the team a wake-up call. It definitely worked. We won the next straight 11 games and capped it off with a Sugar Bowl victory against Penn State.

The '76 season was much different. We lost our opener to Ole Miss 10–7, lost to Georgia 21–0, and lost to Notre Dame 21–18 all on the road. We finished the season 9–3, beating UCLA in the Liberty Bowl. What really stood out about this season was the fact that our fifth game of the year was against Southern Miss in Birmingham, Alabama. We won 24–8. After the game we were in the locker room celebrating when Coach Bryant walked in and said, "You've embarrassed the red jersey today and the tradition of Alabama football. Curfew tonight is 11:00 PM, and be on the field at 8:00 AM. We're going to play this game all over tomorrow. Now let's get dressed and on the buses and head back to Tuscaloosa." We won the game 24–8, but Coach Bryant wanted more. The '77 season was a good one for us, and we went 11–1. Our only loss was the second game of the year to Nebraska 31–24. Once again losing early gave us a chance to redeem ourselves, and we played in the Sugar Bowl against Woody Hayes and Ohio State. We went out and played a solid game, winning 35–6 but fell short of winning the national championship, which went to Notre Dame, who beat Texas in the Cotton Bowl.

The '78 season, my final year wearing the Crimson and White, ended with a national championship. It also ended with the famous goal-line stand against Penn State in the 1979 Sugar Bowl. Going into the game, Penn State was ranked No. 1 with a perfect record of 11–0 while Alabama was ranked No. 2 with a record of 10–1 after losing to USC 24–14 in Week 3. It was a storybook ending to a four-year career of playing for the Crimson Tide. So many things could be said about that game: Nathan ran for over 100 yards, Bruce Bolton caught a long touchdown pass from Rutledge, Don McNeal came off his guy and knocked the receiver out of bounds on second down to prevent a touchdown, and the defense stopped Penn State on third and goal from two yards out. Then came the goal-line stand on fourth and 1.

Timeout was called, and I was standing next to Chuck Fusino, the quarterback for Penn State. I'm not sure he was even talking to me, but he said: "How far is it?" I turned and put my hands apart two feet and said, "About this far."

Fusino's follow-up question was pretty simple: "Well, what do think?"

I replied, "I think you better throw the ball" and ran back to the huddle.

When I got there, Legg was yelling "gut check, gut check." That was a reminder of everything for which Coach Bryant had prepared us. It came down to one play. The defense was signaled in, the ball was snapped, defensive linemen shot the gap, linebackers came over the top, and the corners came off the edge. Everyone did their job. Krauss came over the top and hit the running back as he was coming over the pile, Wingo came from one side, and Legg came from the other side. Mike Clement, our corner, had his legs, and Hannah, our defensive tackle, was in the backfield. It was a great play by Krauss, a great stop by our defense, and a great way to end my season. I probably didn't say thank you enough to all my teammates, coaches, and the fans at the University of Alabama for everything they contributed to my success. You win as a team and you lose a team. Thank you, Bama Nation.

Krauss was one of the most gifted athletes that I played with at the University of Alabama. We competed at everything, including running laps, lifting weights, and, of course, making tackles on the field. It was also friendly competition. Some days I won; some days he won. In the end he made me a better player.

Legg was my roommate for my last two years at Alabama and has remained a friend. To this day he has stayed active in my foundation and more importantly has been a true uncle to my kids. Nathan was the best. The fans labeled him "Touchdown Tony." He never spent a minute on the freshmen field. The day he set foot on campus, he went right to the varsity team. And rightfully so. He was that good. Nathan wasn't just a great football player. He was a better person.

After the season I had the pleasure of representing Alabama in two All-Star games: the East-West Shrine game in San Francisco and the Senior Bowl in Mobile, Alabama. We won both of the games. The interesting part of the Senior Bowl was that we were getting paid, and the second part was that we were actually getting coached by two pro coaching staffs. The South team was being coached by the New Orleans staff, while the North was being coached by the New York Jets staff. I was able to play well enough to be voted the Defensive Player of the Game for the South. Maybe that helped me in the draft.

Before the New York Jets drafted me in the first round 14th overall, I had to tell Coach Bryant I was planning on dropping out of school. This was not a conversation I was looking forward to having. As I entered Coach Bryant's office that morning, he was sitting at his desk smoking a cigarette and waved me into to his office. I thanked him for the opportunity to play at the University of Alabama and told him my plans to drop out of school to get ready for the NFL draft. Coach Bryant was not happy, but he extended his hand and said the following, "Promise me one thing: that one day you'll come back and finish your degree."

We shook hands, and I answered, "Yes sir." Coach Bryant continued saying, "You'll be very fortunate to play a game you love, you'll build financial security for you and your family, but remember this: a winner in the game of life is the person that gives of themselves so others can grow."

Lyons Life Lesson

Life isn't about what you accomplish as an individual; it's about what you share with the people who helped you accomplish your goals.

CHAPTER 3

My Rookie Season
in the NFL

Back in 1979 there was no combine for the players to attend. You worked out on your own, and if an NFL team had interest in you, the team would fly you in for a private workout and physical. I stayed around the campus of the University Alabama and worked out with Barry Krauss, Rich Wingo, and Tony Nathan. We had a routine of running in the morning and lifting weights in the afternoon. I went for physicals with the Jets, Cleveland Browns, Buffalo Bills, and the Tampa Bay Buccaneers. I actually thought my best chance of being drafted was with the Browns. Looking back, those days of working out with Krauss and Wingo were unbelievable, intense, and competitive. Between the three of us, no one wanted to come in last.

Out of all the players drafted into the NFL out of Alabama in 1979, Wingo had the most productive year. With the Green Bay Packers, he was named NFC Defensive Rookie of the Year. His career would be cut short because of injuries, but he found a bigger calling when he turned his life over to Jesus Christ. He was a wild man in college just like the rest of us. But when he became a reborn Christian, he became a mentor to me. While I was still finding my way through life, Wingo had found his platform and purpose. Throughout my life I have been blessed with good friends, and none are more important than Wingo.

The draft wasn't covered like it is today with all the ESPN coverage and whatever. My oldest brother, Jim, actually called me to tell me I was drafted by the Jets before the Jets did. I called my parents and my high school coach, George O'Brien, and jumped a plane to New York filled with excitement but also filled with anxiety, not knowing what to expect. Being a first-round draft choice, expectations were going to be very high from both the Jets' side and also from my side.

The first day of rookie minicamp was pretty typical with physicals, testing, and photos. I remember the Jets wanted a picture with the rookie class, and then they wanted a separate picture with myself; Mark Gastineau, the Jets' second-round pick; and the head coach, Walt

Michaels, with Walt in the middle. He looked at Gastineau and myself and said, "The name of the game is get to the quarterback."

That was the entire conversation. There was no "welcome to the New York Jets." Just get to the quarterback. Coach Michaels was old school. He was all business and not a lot of talk. That's what the NFL was all about. It's a job. You get paid to play football. Training camp was tough. All the rookies, free agents, and some of the returning first-year players reported about two weeks before the veterans. Practices were long and demanding. The Jets were changing their defense from a 3-4 to a 4-3, meaning they were adding a defensive lineman up front. I was expected to start right away. Playing defensive end was a challenge. I really didn't have the speed to turn the corner and get constant pressure on the quarterback. The one thing I learned in college, however, was technique. But technique would only carry you so far in the NFL.

The real highlight of the rookie camp was Gastineau, the second-round draft pick out of East Central Oklahoma. He had the speed to get to quarterback and would get the crowd going by doing a sack dance afterward. He was exciting, but camp took a twist when the veterans reported to practice a few days later. Guys like Greg Buttle and Joe Klecko were going to be on the practice field. Hell, both of them would be in the defensive huddle, telling us what to do. I was very fortunate that Richard Todd was the Jets' starting quarterback in 1979, and we were teammates at Alabama. When Todd was a senior, I was a freshman. So he took me under his wing and showed me the Big Apple. Surprisingly, the other two quarterbacks the Jets had were also from the SEC. Matt Robinson went to Georgia, and Pat Ryan went to Tennessee.

Everyone believed in having a routine. Rookies lifted first and got treatment second. Rookies got in line to get taped for practice. Veterans didn't have to wait; they just cut the line. I couldn't really complain about guys cutting the tape line. I just had to outthink the veterans. So after the first morning practice, I would get iced down, take a shower, and get taped before I went to lunch. It made it even easier for me to take a nap and come over a little later for the afternoon practice.

One of the first veterans I met was Klecko. He was nothing but a big hunk of muscle. He stopped me as I was leaving the weight room and asked me where I was going. I told him I was going home. He asked me if I lifted, and I replied yes. Then he told me that I needed to get stronger to play in the NFL, and I couldn't leave the complex until he did. I replied okay and started to walk off when I heard Klecko bark out, "Where are you going? Didn't you hear me?"

The bark was pretty loud, and I knew I didn't want to feel the bite so I went back in the locker room, changed, and went back in the weight room. That day created a friendship that has lasted more than 40 years. Back in the '70s and '80s, veterans didn't talk with rookies much. It was all about loyalty. There was a good chance that one of their friends, another veteran player, would be cut if draft choices made the team. Klecko was respected by every player on the team. And that 1979 team had a bunch of leaders on it. On the defensive side of the ball, we had guys like Buttle and Abdul Salaam. They gave the pregame speeches, and those speeches were classic. On the offensive side of the ball, there was Todd, Clark Gaines, Marvin Powell, and the old timer, Randy Rassmussen. He was the only player left from Super Bowl III when the Jets beat the Baltimore Colts. Rassmussen taped his hands up and held you even in a walk-through practice when you weren't even in pads.

One of the smartest guys on the defense was Buttle. He knew the entire defense. He knew where everyone was supposed to line up and what everyone's responsibility was. Buttle was an All-American in college from Penn State, and his knowledge showed. If you don't believe me, ask Buttle himself.

During training camp the veterans had a tradition where they took the first-round pick out for drinks and then stuck them with the tab. There were several bars across the street from our training facility: Bill's

Meadowbrook, the Salty Dog, and, of course, Buttle's. That one was owned and operated by Buttle, our starting linebacker. He was very generous at his bar. We ate and drank for free as long as we tipped the bartenders and waitresses. About seven of us also went to the Salty Dog for beers, shots, and a lot of laughs. I guess the veterans got the final laugh. When I excused myself to use the restroom, I returned to the bar, and everyone was gone. The bartender laughed and gave me the tab. He said, "The guys said, 'You were buying today.'" The bill was a couple hundred dollars. I paid it, didn't complain, never said "thanks, guys," and just moved on.

In the years to follow, I was in the middle of some of those future first rounders picking up the tab. Some, if not all, were a lot more than what I paid.

My rookie season roommate was kicker Chuck Ramsey. He was a great guy, but to this day, he probably still has his first Holy Communion money. I remember we went out for breakfast one morning, and the bill was like $23. "It's $15 a piece, which would leave the waitress a $7 tip," I told him.

Then he started up. "Wait a minute," Ramsey said. "You had three eggs; I only had two. You had orange juice. I didn't, and you had English Muffins, and I had toast."

Maybe he had a point. Maybe it was just another veteran trick for me to pick up the entire check, or maybe Ramsey was just cheap. I went with option two and three, though he was serious and convincing. I picked up the entire check, and that was the first and only time Ramsey and I ate together.

After my rookie season, my next roommate was Kenny Schroy. To this day he is one of the most loyal friends anyone could ask for. The Jets went 8–8 my rookie season. We opened up at Shea Stadium against Cleveland. Early in the game, I was playing defensive end when the tight end came to my side. The No. 1 rule was not to get hooked by the tight end and to make sure to hold the edge. My old college teammate, Ozzie Newsome, was the tight end. I lined up in a wide nine position to hold the edge when Newsome looked up and said, "What's up, homie?" I started to reply. Then the ball was snapped, Newsome hooked me, and the running back ran for about 15 yards around my side. Lesson learned: hellos are for after the game not during the game. Newsome is in both the College Football and Pro Football Hall of Fame. He was a great football player, but he's a better man.

The next week we didn't play any better, losing to the New England Patriots 56–3. Yes, this was the NFL, and this was the Jets at our worst. The score was 35–3 at halftime, and the fans in Foxboro were outright nasty. The front row of the stadium was so close to the bench that the fans seemed like they were right on top of us. They called our mothers, wives, and sisters by every name in the book. I couldn't believe how creative they were. Some of the comments were outright funny. The more points New England scored, the louder they got. Buttle gave the best advice: "Don't acknowledge them."

After the game the locker room was bitterly quiet. What was someone supposed to say? We sucked. It was a terrible game by all, including the coaches. Once we got back to the airport, the flight attendants were standing outside the plane handing out a plastic bag with two beers in it. Wow, this was an eye opener. *Beer supplied by the NFL after a game?* Nice! The cool thing about this was when you became a veteran player, the routine continued, and you sat in the same seat every week, and the flight attendant had your beer on ice. So the motto was created: "win or lose, you always had your booze."

Somewhere in the middle of season, we were playing a home game when a fight broke out. I reacted by getting into the scrum and grabbed Klecko from behind in a bear hug and pulled him out. After getting back to the huddle, Klecko looked at me and said, "If you ever do that again,

I'll kick your ass right here in front of everyone. You either fight with me or leave me the fuck alone."

This was game-changing moment for me. This wasn't college football anymore. If you got into a fight on the football field at that level, Coach Bryant would help you pack your bags and send you home. Fighting wasn't necessary in the NFL, but it was acceptable. Good ol' Klecko. I had a teammate who was going to make me a better player, a teammate who would always have my back. It doesn't get any better than that.

Lining up against quarterbacks that I watched on TV for so many years was not only exciting for a rookie, but also scary. The AFC East had four of the better quarterbacks: Bob Griese for the Miami Dolphins, Bert Jones for the Colts, Joe Ferguson for the Bills, and Steve Grogan for the Patriots. I met Griese for the first time in 1975 when I was honored with the Amateur Athlete of the Year award by the *St. Petersburg Times*, and he was the keynote speaker that night. His message was simple. He told all the award winners to use that honor as a steppingstone to our next award. He said to feel good about tonight's awards, but move on to your next goal.

Jones had a rifle of an arm, and the Colts were still in Baltimore. It seemed we always matched up with the Colts well. Ferguson was tougher than nails. No matter how many times you hit him, he just kept lining up. Grogan seemed like the thorn in the Jets' side. He would come out looking like Jack Lambert of the Pittsburgh Steelers, wearing pads everywhere, a neck roll, and knee braces. He was one of the best. Jets fans, as well all as players, won't ever forget the September 9 game in 1979 when Grogan threw for five touchdowns and no interceptions against us.

Also, I was able to line up against Terry Bradshaw. He was the guy in the NFL winning all those Super Bowls in the 1970s. He was also a good guy. When I had my first football camp in Alabama, he and Archie Manning were kind enough to attend.

Mid-December was rolling in, my rookie season was coming to an end, and Christmas parties were starting to take place. I saw a notice on the bulletin board in the locker room that said "Long Island Leukemia Christmas Party." It had a sign-up sheet for players to attend that already had two names, Pat Leahy and Schroy, on it. So I decided to add my name on the list. Who would have known that the Long Island Leukemia Christmas Party would change my life forever?

Who knew that this one sign-up sheet would lead me to participate in annual Christmas parties to help sick kids? I still cherish these events. (Marty Lyons Foundation)

The season ended, post-season physicals were taken, and then players left. Some even left directly after the game. Quick good-byes and "See ya at minicamp" was the extent of a lot of the conversion. Michaels was tough but respected. With the players that we had in the locker room and the coaches on Michaels' staff, I couldn't wait to see what next season was going to bring.

With my rookie season coming to a close, I was getting to start a new chapter in my life. I was getting married in January to my college girlfriend, Kelley. She was from a small town in Alabama called Demopolis. She came to New York a couple of times during my rookie season. Kelly was also finishing up her college degree. It was a long-distance relationship, and the marriage failed eight years later when Kelley filed for a divorce. God blessed us with a beautiful son, Rocky, who was born in 1982. I blame myself for the divorce. I should have been a better husband. Looking back now, I had priorities in the wrong order. They were a little out of whack. I moved my career in front of family and faith.

Lyons Life Lesson

Family is a term that includes people who believe in the same values and goals that you do.

CHAPTER 4
The Early 1980s

The theme and the buzz in the building after the 1979 season was to rebuild, refocus, pick up where we ended in 1979, and then start fast. We did everything but that, losing our first five games.

The defensive line had a completely different look. Switching positions with Joe Klecko, I got moved from right defensive end to right defensive tackle. Abdul Salaam stayed at left tackle, and Mark Gastineau earned the left defensive end starting role. That gave us two guys who could turn the corner and get constant pressure on the quarterback. The draft class of 1980 was also productive. First-round pick Johnny Lam Jones, a wide receiver out of Texas, could fly. He was so fast you didn't see his feet hit turf as he ran. He had won a gold medal in the 4x100 meter relay at the 1976 Olympics in Montreal. He perfectly complemented our other wide receiver, Wesley Walker, who was special. He could run, catch, and was great in the locker room. We also drafted a safety out of Oklahoma named Darrol Ray. He was a smart, hard-hitting safety with great speed. But the diamond in the rough was Lance Mehl, our third-round pick out of Penn State. Mehl was a student of the game. What he didn't learn at Penn State he was about to learn from Greg Buttle. The only thing that could derail Mehl were injuries. Making it through the long season and staying healthy was the key for most players in the NFL. There's a big difference between being hurt and being injured. In the '80s you found yourself playing through the pain because there was always someone waiting to take your place. The trainers and doctors always had the right medication ready if you wanted to play.

The entire Jets organization was disappointed when we ended the season 4–12. How bad were we? There were only two other teams, the New York Giants and the Seattle Seahawks, who finished 4–12. The only other team worse than the Jets that season were the New Orleans Saints, and they were 1–15. Their only win that season came against us. They beat us 21–20 in late December at Shea Stadium. Sadly, we would have to start all over in the offseason and go back to the drawing board.

Once again, the Long Island Leukemia Christmas Party was taking place. Usually, the same guys showed up and took turns being Santa Claus. That year's party was special. I met the shyest, neatest kid named Keith. The kid, who was 4½, had leukemia. He was beautiful. He had blond hair and a smile that just captured my heart. I didn't have any children of mine own at the time. Unbeknownst to me at that time, Keith would become a key player in my life. As I got ready to leave the party that day, I went over to Keith's mother, Susan, and gave her my information and asked her if I could stay in contact with her and Keith. The highlight of the event was when Keith came over jumped in my arms and said, "I love you." My heart melted.

These kids were special. They knew their fight with cancer was going to take a lot of treatment. They weren't afraid. They didn't care whether the Jets won or lost. They taught us about facing life with faith. They weren't afraid of dying and, though they wanted to live, they knew they were there for a reason. Keith changed my purpose in life. We fought his disease together through treatments both at Long Island Jewish Hospital and at Sloane Kettering in New York City. The next 15 months, Keith and Susan had their highs and lows in life. On March 10, 1982, Keith passed away two months shy of his sixth birthday.

It's important to take time to reflect on life. People come in and out of our lives, and some make an impact, and some just make an impression. God allows this to happen as a test to see who will take time to listen. You can actually learn more by listening than talking sometimes. I've learned a lot about myself in the last 50 years from others and also my own mistakes. We all can make a difference in life if we take time to care. Don't judge people on who they were 20, 30 years ago. Judge them for who they are today. For example, I went back for my 25th high school reunion and had a chance to see some old familiar faces. I ran into that left fielder who that had the ball bounce off his face. He came right up to me and asked why we always made fun of him. I knew it was true. So

I stuck my hand out and said I was sorry that I wasn't the person that I am today when I was 18. He shook my hand, said thank you, and walked off. He had been carrying that hurt for 25 years.

* * *

Every year in the NFL is different. Before the season ever starts, everyone believes you're going to win your division and win the Super Bowl. Adding to the optimism was that we drafted Freeman McNeil out of UCLA with our first-round pick. McNeil was outstanding. He could run the rock up the middle and had the speed to bounce the ball outside. McNeil was a true professional both on and off the field. When he spoke to the team, it was strong, passionate, and commanding. What people don't know about McNeil was he stood up against the NFL about a program called Plan B free agency system, which helped usher in the rules of free agency that exist today. To this day, McNeil is loved by his former teammates and loved by the Jets Nation.

The defensive line was something special. Later that season we were nicknamed "the New York Sack Exchange." But it wasn't just the play of the defensive line. The entire defense was better. Despite all of the positive things that surrounded the team, we still started the season 0–3. Somehow we turned the season around and finished 10–5–1 and earned a spot in the playoffs. Our playoff game was against the Buffalo Bills at Shea Stadium. The fans were ready for the game, and so were we. Buffalo kicked off. Our return man had the ball at the 5, at the 10, and reached the 20 when he got hit and fumbled. Buffalo picked up the fumble and returned it for a touchdown. I remember looking up at the game clock, and 15 seconds into the game, we were down by seven points. The crowd kept us in the game as we fought back, but we were denied on the final drive by an interception in the end zone. We lost 31–27, and the season was over just like that.

I hang out with my former New York Sack Exchange linemates in January of 2020. From left to right, it's me, Joe Klecko, and Mark Gastineau, and in front of us is Abdul Salaam.

That '81 season was a lot of fun and so was being part of the New Your Sack Exchange. The approach we had wasn't if we were going to get the quarterback. It was how many times were we going to get him. The Jets had two of the best pass rushers in the game: Mark Gastineau and Joe Klecko. They both had strength and speed and yet they played the game so differently. Klecko was a brown-paper-bag-type of guy. Gastineau was more flamboyant and was known for his sack dances. Klecko was a leader not just for the defense, but also for the entire team. He told me I better be prepared to play both mentally and physically and that I better not take the field if that wasn't the case. If you're not ready to play, you'll get hurt or—even worse—get one of your teammates hurt.

Being a part of the Sack Exchange brings back many good memories. We went to the New York Stock Exchange and rang the opening bell. All the traders on the floor stopped making money for their clients and took pictures and asked for autographs. At the end of the day, we put on our Jets uniforms and took a group shot on the floor of the exchange.

When Klecko worked a shoe deal with Pro Keds for the four of us, we used that photo for the poster. None of us were wearing Pro Keds that day. The company just super imposed the shoes on our feet. The best part of the shoe deal was getting sweat suits, T-shirts, and running shoes in all different sizes. My house looked like a sporting goods store. And yes, the money was okay also. I got shoes for the entire football team at my old high school and took care of some needy families in Alabama.

Our front four was special, but the back seven of the Jets also did an excellent job in coverage to allow us time to get to the quarterback. Greg Buttle, Lance Mehl, Kenny Schroy, Bobby Jackson, and Darrol Ray were outstanding. The defensive coordinator was Joe Gardi, and he just turned the defensive loose. He would signal in the defense, and if Buttle didn't like it, he'd yell back to the sideline, "That didn't work the last time." And he'd change the call. I have to hand it to him. Most of the time he was right, and, secondly, it took a lot of balls to do that.

That '81 team was very close. We did a lot on off-the-field stuff together. From Buttle's bar to Klecko's bar, we had plenty of places to go. After all the home games at Shea Stadium, we always went to Patrick's Pub right down the street from the stadium, where we unwound with family members over drinks and food.

My wife and I were expecting our first child in 1982. Keith was moved from Long Island Jewish Hospital to Sloane Kettering in New York City. On Tuesdays, which was the players' day off, I spent the day with him. He was in an isolated room, where you had to put on surgical scrubs before going in. Schroy and I donated blood and platelets in Keith's name. Schroy didn't have to do this, but that was the kind of person he was, and that showed the type of friendship we had. Keith was fighting for his life.

Kevin Turner was another fighter. I met him at my Marty Lyons Camp of Champions. I was very fortunate to have my own football camp in Marion, Alabama, and it was my way of giving back football knowledge to young athletes who enjoyed football. The best coaches were players that I played with like college teammates Barry Krauss, Rich Wingo, and NFL teammates like Klecko, Schroy, and Joe Fields. Turner was 10 or 11, and you could see he was born to play the game. He developed into a leader that one day would take him to the University of Alabama. An outstanding fullback and gifted blocker, he ended up playing for the New England Patriots and Philadelphia Eagles. I was so proud of him for becoming the man he was. After an eight-year career in the NFL and countless concussions, he retired. In March of 2016, Turner died of ALS. Before his death he used his platform to bring awareness to that disease. Turner made an impact in life.

Lyons Life Lesson

If you have real faith, don't fear dying. Faith is believing in something you can't see. But if you have enough faith, when you die, you'll be rewarded in seeing everything that you believed in.

It's never too late to say you're sorry. You can always make more money, but you can't make more time so treasure it, respect it, and share it.

CHAPTER 5
The Tragic 1982 Season

The excitement from the '81 season carried over. The New York Sack Exchange was getting booked left and right for photo opts, signings, and personal appearances. I was on top of the world. Life couldn't get any better. My wife was expecting in early March, and Keith was still fighting. All that would change in the first week of March.

On March 4 my son, Rocky, was born. He's really Martin Anthony Jr., but my mother-in-law, Maxine, gave him the nickname Rocky minutes after he was born. I called to tell my parents of their grandson and told my dad that we were bringing home Rocky on March 7 and that I would call him that night. He said he would check into flights and I could pick him up on March 8. I called my dad up to see what time he was coming in, got the information, and ended the conversion by saying, "I love you, Dad. I'll see you tomorrow."

Rocky's first night at home was a long one. He was crying and hungry. I remember changing him and giving him a bottle somewhere around 5:00 AM, got him settled in his crib, and went back to bed. I wasn't back in bed for even an hour when the house phone rang. It was my sister, Theresa, telling me that Dad had a heart attack in his sleep and that I needed to get down there. So I went to the bank to get some money, and when I returned, my wife told me that she had gotten a follow-up call saying that my dad had passed away. The day I was supposed to pick him up to see his grandson, I was flying down for his funeral.

On March 10, as my family gathered at the funeral home for my father's wake, I had a strange feeling come to me. I excused myself and went outside. I had to call home. I gave my wife an update from Florida on my dad and followed up with the question: "How's Keith?" The phone went silent. I still remember my wife's words: "He died this morning."

How could this happen? What was I doing so wrong in my life that God would bless me with a healthy son and then four days later take my father and then two days later take Keith. I was 25 years old. This wasn't supposed to happen to me. Why me?

Rocky, who was born during a tragic period in my life, hangs out with me in the Jets' locker room.

My first phone call was to Susan, Keith' mom. She knew the pain I was feeling, and I knew the pain she was in. My second call was to Kenny Schroy. Talking through tears, I told him what had happened and asked him to attend Keith's funeral on my behalf, and he and his wife did.

This was that moment that Coach Bryant had prepared me for back in 1979. It was my time to use my platform. I didn't know how, but the moment was real.

* * *

The 1982 season came with the excitement that the Jets had drafted Bob Crable in the first round from Notre Dame. He was a hard-nosed football player with a high football IQ. He fit perfectly with Greg Buttle and Lance Mehl. Unfortunately for the Jets and for Crable, his career was cut short by injuries, and he played only six years. We drafted Reggie McElroy, a big-bodied offensive tackle, that same year, and he developed into a pretty good NFL player who played 13 years. And that same year we drafted Rocky Klever out of Montana. Klever was a man of all trades. If you needed a tight end, Klever was the guy. You needed a scout-team quarterback, Klever was the guy. If you needed someone to make you laugh, Klever was the guy.

During a preseason game against the New York Giants, he had a stomach virus and had been throwing up all day and was suffering though diarrhea. Klever was on the field that hot August night, running a crossing route when he got crushed by one of the Giants linebackers. There was an explosion on the field—and also in Rocky's pants. Klever *literally* got the crap knocked out of him. The offense punted, and the defense took the field, and Klever was circled by the training staff, who were cleaning him up by putting a clean pair of football pants on him and throwing the dirty, crappy towels under the bench. Well, when the defense came off the field, I just happened to be sitting on the bench yelling at the trainers for water and a towel. I looked down saw a towel, picked it up, and started to wipe my face with it. I stopped a few seconds later because of the smell, but I had it everywhere—even in my beard. As the trainers laughed, I got pissed, but there was nothing I could do but rinse my face off.

The preseason also featured the end of the line for John Nitti's Jets career. He might not be recognized by a lot of Jets fans because he's a perfect example of a player who struggled to stay healthy during his entire NFL career. He was an outstanding running back at Yale, which tells you right away that Nitti was smart, very smart. He came to the Jets in 1981 as a free agent running back with the toughness to be a strong safety. During the first practice at training camp, Nitti hurt his knee, which meant that Nitti's season was over and that he would spend entire season on injury reserve. Nitti was the type of player who fit right in with the veteran players, so a few of us took him under our wings as he did his rehab in hopes to make it back for the 1982 season.

The 1982 season rolled around, and Nitti was probably in the best shape of his life. He worked out with the defensive backs, doing sprint work, and hit the weight room daily. Then in early to mid-August during training camp, he broke his leg, and his season was over. Once again he was heading to injured reserve. Being a proud man, Nitti went to the Jets and told them he couldn't expect to get paid for a second year without earning money. We thought John was nuts. *Take the money. You earned it the day you got hurt.* Though he later spent time in the Giants camp and with the New Jersey Generals of the USFL, his career ended at the age of 26 due to injuries. He had the will of a champion but couldn't stay healthy. He played for the love of the game—not the money he expected to earn. Nitti was just one of many NFL players who didn't get to show case their talent due to injuries. But he took his Yale education to Wall Street and had a very successful career.

The 1982 season was a strike year. The players sat out for a total of 57 days. A lot of the players got part-time jobs. Kenny Schroy and I went to work for a local electronics company in Hempstead, New York. We did some sales for them but found ourselves counting inventory most of the time. The pay wasn't great, but it was something to put in your pocket. The NFL decided to shorten the season from 16 games to nine and have a 16-team playoff from each conference. The Jets finished the year 6–3— good enough for a wild-card spot. All the games would be on the road, starting with the Bengals in Cincinnati.

The week leading up to the game, Walt Michaels walked into the meeting room, slapped down $5,000 in cash on the podium, and said, "There's $5,000 here. Do you want this?" He paused before saying, "Then win." His speech fired us up. The $5,000 was the winning share that every player got if we won the wild-card game, and what a game it was. Freeman McNeil ran for more than 200 yards, the defense put pressure on quarterback Kenny Anderson all day, and we walked away with a 44–17 victory. The next stop was playing the Raiders in Oakland.

Coach Michaels kept the theme going. For the Oakland week, he brought in $10,000, the winning share per player if we won the divisional playoff game. Prior to the game, as I was getting ready to get the team fired up to take the field and yelling and screaming about what we had to do to win the game, I slammed my fist through a painted white glass window. At the time I didn't know it was a window. I actually thought it was a piece of plywood painted white. I pulled my arm of the window and saw it was covered in blood. The trainers Bob Reese and Pepper Burruss followed me out onto the field with a towel. Blood didn't matter that day. We were playing the Raiders on their turf and we were in for a dogfight. The only way to win a dogfight is to have everyone—offense, defense, and special teams—on the same page and doing their jobs. As the game played out, Richard Todd connected with Wesley Walker for a score, Mehl came up with a couple of interceptions, and the team played with confidence. We won 17–14.

That win got us a spot in the AFC Championship Game, and we had to play the Miami Dolphins in the Orange Bowl, their home stadium. We lost both of our regular-season games to the Dolphins. We lost our Week One opener to them 45–28 and then lost 20–19 in the Orange Bowl in Week Seven. After winning back-to-back playoff road games, we were pretty confident that Miami wasn't going to beat us three times in the same season.

With one game to go to the Super Bowl, Coach Michaels was true to himself and his team. He slapped $15,000 in cash on the podium and asked, "Do you want this?" We didn't just want it; we worked for it. But that whole week it rained in Miami. The field was left uncovered, and the game was labeled the "Mud Bowl." Any time you play in the conditions that we played in that day, the game is going to be played at a slow pace.

With the field being in the condition that it was, Todd threw five interceptions. That plus poor play by the defense led to a 14–0 loss. A lot was said after that game about the conditions of the field. But it wasn't like we played on the wet field, and every time the Dolphins got the ball, they went to a dry field. Todd had a bad day and he'll be the first one to admit to that. But if it wasn't for his play in the two previous games, we wouldn't have even been in this game. Football is a team sport. We lost that day as a team—not because of the field or one person's performance. Miami was a better team that day. Hell, we ended the season going 8–4, losing to Miami three times They had our number that year, but we had something special building for the future with the guys in the locker room and the coaching staff Michaels had under him.

After the game the locker room was quiet. Owner Leon Hess came around and congratulated every player for an outstanding season. You don't ever get over a loss like that. You just learn to live with it. We got on the plane to fly back to New York, and there was one guy, Michaels, who was really pissed off. He was mad at the league for not mandating that the field was covered during the week of rain. He was mad at Don Shula because he thought the head coach of the Dolphins had something to do with not covering the field. Michaels was fighting for every one of his players, and there was no calming him down.

To the surprise of the players, Michaels didn't show up at the meeting the next day. Joe Walton, the offensive coordinator, came in and said, "Good season, men. See you next year." Wherever Michaels was remains a mystery to this day.

Michaels was fired within the next couple of weeks. As far as the players were concerned, he was our guy and he was standing up for us, the organization, and the fans. Whatever he said or did, we felt he didn't deserve to be fired.

When Michaels was fired, we also lost some fine assistant coaches like Bob Fry and Dan "Sink" Sekanovich. We lost our running back coach Bob Ledbetter to the Giants coaching staff. Coach Ledbetter, who was the best, died in October of 1983 after suffering a stroke in September. He didn't just develop players like McNeil and Bruce Harper, but he also developed a friendship with all the players. Even though Ledbetter was taken away from us way to early, he had an impact on all of our lives.

Instead of picking up where we left off after barely missing the Super Bowl, the 1983 season would now be a mystery with a new head coach, Joe Walton.

I really struggled for answers in 1982—more so about life than football. Days turned into weeks, weeks turned into months, and I couldn't bring back my father or Keith. One morning I woke up and didn't like the reflection I saw in the mirror. Death had changed me into someone I wasn't proud of, someone who both my father and Keith would have been disappointed in. I reached out to my teammate and best friend, Schroy, for help. I explained to him that I wanted to start a foundation in memory of my father and Keith to help terminally ill children. I wanted to take their greatest wish in life and make it become a reality. I wanted them to feel important just like I did every time I took the football field. Schroy was on board 100 percent, but I needed outside help to figure out how to fund a not-for-profit foundation.

My dad's brother, Bob, lived in East Meadow, Long Island. After a couple of meetings discussing the foundation, he introduced me to a man named Bill Gibney, who worked with Hempstead Bank and found it in his heart to help me under one condition. This foundation was not going to be a one-and-done foundation. Gibney emphasized the word commitment over and over again. He wanted to make sure I was 100 percent in. I was.

By the end of the calendar year in 1982, the Marty Lyons Foundation was born. We were licensed as a 501(c) nonprofit organization in the State of New York.

Now it was time to raise money and provide a special wish to a special child suffering with a terminal illness. Going into 1983, I knew the only way to raise money was to raise awareness of childhood cancer. So I decided that for every speaking engagement I did, I would donate the fee back to the foundation. I found myself telling complete strangers the story of my son being born just before losing my father and Keith. I told them I needed their help to raise money. It was then that I found out just how generous people really were. After I left the speaking engagements, people handed me checks, cash, and business cards and said they wanted to get involved to support me on my mission. I even had an insurance broker donate office space with one of his assistants to help run the everyday operation. Soon I had the funding to grant our first wish.

But my year didn't get any easier.

On January 26, 1983, I was sitting at my house in Melville, Long Island, when an ABC News flash hit the screen. I'll never forget the announcement, saying, "Just in from Tuscaloosa, Alabama, the legendary Paul 'Bear' Bryant has died of a massive heart attack." A lump developed in my throat, and tears began running down my face. I couldn't believe my ears. Coach Bryant, the one person who had more influence on my life than anyone I've ever came into connect with, had died. I remember flying to Birmingham, Alabama, and then going to Tuscaloosa for his funeral. Hundreds of thousands of people attended. Those who could not get into the church listened to the services that were piped to the street, which were stacked three rows deep with people. The motorcade was at least five miles long, heading back to Birmingham. Every overpass was lined with people, and some held signs, but all paid respect to a man they loved, a man that had an impact on their lives. I loved Coach Bryant— not for the lessons he taught me on the football field, but the lessons that he taught me in life. I continue to use them today, sharing them with the strangers I meet.

Lyons Life Lesson

Isn't it amazing that we can remember the day that someone dies but can't remember a birthday or someone's anniversary? That's because when you lose someone they take a part of your heart with them. To continue in our journey, we must take a part of them with us because time will not stop for anyone of us to heal.

A 17-year-old boy named Jonathan told me to share his experience with cancer. He said to live life to its fullest each and every day because life will be short, no matter how long you live.

CHAPTER 6
Hiring Joe Walton and Leaving Shea Stadium

Joe Walton was a hell of an offensive coordinator. The question then was: what kind of head coach would he be? The 1983 draft was coming up and it was loaded with talent, especially at the quarterback position. John Elway, Jim Kelly, Todd Blackledge, Tony Eason, Dan Marino, and Kenny O'Brien were all predicted to go in the first round. Rumor had it that the Jets were going to draft a quarterback in the first round to learn from Richard Todd and—as it is in the NFL—then eventually take over for him. They drafted O'Brien with the 24th pick right in front of Marino, who was taken by the Miami Dolphins.

O'Brien had a lot of talent. He could really spin the ball. He had a strong arm and could make all the NFL throws expected out of an NFL quarterback. The Jets also selected Johnny Hector, a running back out of Texas A&M in the second round. This move solidified the backfield and helped Freeman McNeil out. The third-round pick was Jo Jo Townsell, a wide receiver out of UCLA. Townsell also was used a return specialist. And in ninth round, they selected Bobby Humphrey, a defensive back out of New Mexico. You always knew where you stood with the organization after the draft. If they drafted players at your position, that was not a good thing.

The first two seasons under Walton were tough. The chemistry we had as a team had splintered after the firing of Michaels. Walton wasn't like Michaels at all. Michaels was old school and told it like it was. If you didn't like it, don't let the door hit you on your ass on the way out. Walton, well, he was a politician. He wanted to be liked by all and at the same time respected by all. For Walton to have both, he had to control the team both on and off the field and control of all the different personalities. Controlling the personalities was going to be more difficult than getting the gameplan correct.

Walton had a good coaching staff, starting with a guy named Mike Faulkiner. A quarterback coach before moving to the defensive side, he was one of the guys. On Fridays we had shortened practices where we just reviewed game situations. Faulkiner always had a habit of wanting to be the first off the field, first in his car, and the first to leave the complex. As Faulkiner ran off the field, the players would still be huddling with their individual coaches, and, of course, Faulkiner would give us all that one finger wave, jump in his car, and take off. So I played a joke on him. Coach Faulkiner had an old, beat-up car and always parked it in the same space against the fence. Well, I decided to go under his car and tape a military smoke bomb to his car. I then proceeded to take some fishing line and tie it from the pin to the fence. So when Faulkiner backed out roughly 10 to 15 seconds later, the car would be engulfed in smoke. Sure enough, the plan worked. Practice finished, and Faulkiner ran off the field, gave us the one finger wave, jumped in car, backed up, and the fun started. He got through the Jets security gate when the smoke bomb engulfed his whole car. As we stood there and laughed, all we could hear was Faulkiner yelling, "Get back. I think it's going to blow." We couldn't stop laughing as we all gave him the one finger wave.

The other member of Walton's staff who was a classic was our strength and conditioning coach Jim Williams. He liked to spell his name "Gym," not Jim. He was good at what he did, but he was an easy target. When we reported back to camp, there were drills that we had to do: a mile run, vertical jump, four-corner drill, 40-yard run, and bench press. I thought, *let's start the season off with a bang*. The mile run was simple. You lined up on the track, ran around it four times, and then it was over. It was no problem for me. I loved running distance ever since I was a kid. But as Joe Klecko once said, "If I have to chase a running back a mile, he's got a good chance of scoring." The next test was the vertical jump. You took one step, jumped as high as you could, and then slapped the plastic measuring sticks at the top. So that's what I did except I taped tongue depressors to my right hand, jumped, yelled as if I hurt my hand, and then pulled the tongue depressors (which gave me added height) off and waited. Williams asked me if I was okay, told me I actually jumped six inches higher than last year, and that all was good. I wasn't done with him. I was just getting started. Next was the bench press, where you benched 225 pounds as many times as you could. Kicker Pat Leahy was right before me, and we changed the weights to 200 pounds. Leahy probably could do that weight one time, but with me spotting him, he got it eight or nine times. Williams said to change the weights back to 225 pounds. It was my turn.

So I banged the weights around, reshuffled them a little, and got in position to lift. Williams looked at the weight and gave me the green light. I pumped out around 40 to 45 reps. Williams said it was great that I did six more reps then I did last year. What Williams didn't realize was that during all of the changing and banging of the weights from Leahy's 200 pounds, I actually put it back on 200 pounds. Getting away with the first two drills on Coach Williams was easy, but the third and final one—the 40-yard dash—would be tough.

This year Williams wanted to time the player in the five-yard dash to also find our explosion speed. He actually went out and bought a device that hooked up to the back of your shirt. You popped the cord for a timing device. When it was my turn, I took the cord, wrapped it around my body once, and snapped it to my shirt. The clock started when you made your first move, the cord pulled the pin for the timing device at five yards, and then you continued to run the rest of the 35 yards. But the way I had the cord wrapped around my body, it snapped at three yards instead of five, which meant my time was coming in faster than Wesley Walker and Al Toon. Williams couldn't figure it out, so he had me run again. Again I did the same thing with the same results. That was it for that timing machine. Williams deemed it broken. Make no mistake about it: Williams was one of the better strength and conditioning coaches in the NFL, even though I got a few pranks past him.

In 1983 the Jets went 7–9. It was like being on a roller coaster. We'd win one, loss two, win two, loss three. We weren't a team on the same page. Life in the NFL is about building one season and picking up where you left off to be better than the year before. But we didn't do that.

Let me say this about playing games at Shea Stadium: the locker room was a dump. It probably had six to eight showers, and only four or five worked. At that time the only worse locker rooms that I can remember were in Cleveland and Baltimore. The reason was they shared stadiums with their home baseball teams: the New York Mets, Baltimore Orioles, and the Cleveland Indians. When playing a home game at Shea Stadium, the normal routine was to get in the locker room two hours before the game, but there was about six or seven of us that always got there about three to three-and-a-half hours before the game. Back then we didn't have headsets with music. One of us would bring a boom box in and play music until the rest of the team reported. Someone brought in this oversized boom box, and the music was playing at level six. I had just gotten taped up and was sitting in front of my locker listening to the music while drinking a cup of coffee and enjoying a dip of tobacco when the coach's office down the hall opened. Out came Walton chewing on his cigar. He was pissed off that the music was playing. So he headed over to the boom box, shut the music off, and went back in his office. What was that all about? So I went back over to the boom box and cranked the music up to level eight or nine and walked back to my locker. Meanwhile Pat Ryan, the backup quarterback, was coming out of the trainer's room and stopped to look at this oversized boom box. Ryan had his back to coach's office when that door flew out again. Walton was fuming. He had just shut the music off about 10 minutes before. That's when I yelled over to Ryan to turn the music down. Ryan turned around to see Walton as he said, "Pat, you might not be playing, but some guys are getting ready to play. Now turn that crap off."

Ryan looked at me like *what just happened?* Ryan just happened to be in the wrong place at the wrong time. He had nothing to do with the volume of the music, and the music had nothing to do with us winning or losing. It wasn't about what the players wanted three hours before the game. It was all about the control that Walton wanted to have or thought he had. Well, changes were on their way.

After the 1983 season, the first member of the New York Sack Exchange, Abdul Salaam, was traded to the San Diego Chargers along with Kenny Neil. I hated to see Salaam go. He was the individual who kept the front four on the same page. When you talk about different personalities, the four of us didn't always socialize with each other off the field. But come game time, it was different; we all knew that we needed each other for the team to win.

Scott Dierking, our running back, was released after the season, and the big shocker came in February of 1984 when the Jets traded Todd to the New Orleans Saints. When I look back at what Todd did—or didn't do—for the Jets, his expectation was tainted by the New York media. With Todd coming from Alabama and playing for Coach Bryant, there was a perception that the Jets had another Joe Namath. But there is only one Namath and there will never be another. They needed to let Todd be his own guy. But the Jets drafted O'Brien in 1983. That's business in the NFL. I didn't know when, but my day would come as well because very few players will ever escape the NFL process.

Those early 1980s Jets teams had some great players, and many ended their careers on other teams. Clark Gaines was a tough running back and a great receiver out of the backfield. He was one of my first friends on the Jets. We were neighbors who lived in New York during both the season and offseason. After my rookie season, I went to back to Alabama, but then I bought my first house in New York in 1980, and that's when I was neighbors with Gaines. I remember doing autograph sessions with him and seeing him sign pictures to kids with "See ya in the NFL." I thought that was the greatest thing you could write. When Gaines left the Jets to finish his career, I adopted that saying onto my pictures for kids.

Matt Robinson was one of the coolest guys on the team. He ended up getting traded to the Denver Broncos after a long competition with Todd for the starting position. Many would say that Robinson actually won that competition, but in the end, Todd stayed, and Robinson was gone. We played the Broncos that next preseason, and Robinson took us out for dinner and paid the tab. That meant we drank more and ordered the biggest steaks. When the bill came, Robinson whipped out his credit card and gave it to the waitress—only to find out the only credit card he had was expired. So Robinson got us again. We ended up treating him to dinner.

Joe Fields was an undersized offensive lineman, but he was a smart player. Whatever he lacked in size, he made up with the knowledge of the game. Fields went to a couple of Pro Bowls and was a leader of the team until he was cut and ended his career with the New York Giants.

One of the all-time best offensive lineman the Jets ever had, Marvin Powell was a No. 1 pick in 1977 out of USC. Powell was both smart and a very physical player. The battles between him and Mark Gastineau were classic every day. Powell made Gastineau a better player and he represented the Jets in five Pro Bowls.

To this day I believe that Mickey Shuler was the best all-around tight end that the Jets have had in the last 40 years. He wasn't fast, but if you wanted him to block, he could block. If you asked Shuler to run a five-yard out, he ran it to a T. Coming out of Penn State, he was a student of the game. He ended his career with the Philadelphia Eagles.

John Roman was big, tall, and strong. He was probably the strongest guy on the team in the early '80s, but he couldn't stay healthy. His career was cut short by injuries.

Guy Bingham was an overachiever. He came into the league in 1980 as a 10th-round draft pick. What made Bingham so valuable to the team was that he was the best long snapper in the league, and he learned to play all three positions on the offensive line: guard, tackle, and center. He was another valuable player who ended his career with another team and played 14 years in the league.

A kicker in the NFL sometimes finds himself isolated, all alone on the sideline waiting for that big kick. But Leahy was one of us. We all loved him. What he meant to the Jets was instant points, and he spent 18 years as a kicker for one team. That's almost unheard of. Leahy made 71 percent of his field goals, 96 percent of his extra points, and scored 1,470 points. He played soccer in college and he played in four NCAA soccer finals, won three national championships, and was an All-American. I'm proud to call him a friend and was happy to see him retire as a member of the New York Jets family.

Drafted as a defensive tackle in 1977 out of LSU, Dan Alexander—or Cajun, as some of us called him—was tougher than nails. The guy never missed a game and hardly ever missed a practice. He played 13 years with the Jets and was one of those guys who let his play do the talking.

Drafted in the sixth round in 1978 out of Florida State, Bobby Jackson was a physical corner who could match up one on one with the opposing team's No. 1 receiver. He also talked a good game from start to finish. If you needed a trash talker on the field, Jackson was the best and he could back it up. He ended his career with the Jets in 1983 with 21 career interceptions.

Lawrence Pillers or Booba took me under his wing my rookie season. He was a little bit crazy, a little bit wild, but he could play. Booba was replaced by Gastineau and went to the San Francisco 49ers where he won two Super Bowl rings.

Teddy Banker might not be a name that jumps off the page for Jets fans. Banker was an offensive guard out of Southeast Missouri State who played for the Jets from 1983 to 1988 and later played for the Cleveland Browns from 1989 to 1991. I got into a fight almost every day with Banker because he ran the scout team. He was a solid player who went hard every single play. If you slanted outside and beat Banker, he'd cut you at knees or pull you down by the back of your jersey. It didn't matter what he had to do. You were not going to make the play.

* * *

After the '83 season, it was announced that the Jets were leaving Shea Stadium and were going to New Jersey to play our home games at Giants Stadium. There was something unique about playing at Shea and playing your early home games on the clay infield of the baseball field. Yes, Shea was dated, and the locker rooms needed a facelift, but the atmosphere was unbelievable with planes flying over the stadium after taking off at LaGuardia Airport.

We played our last game of the season in 1981 against the Green Bay Packers. When we won, the fans stormed the field after a 28–3 win to tear down the goal post because we had just earned a spot in the play-off as a wild-card team. The following week we played the Buffalo Bills, and when we were coming from behind on our final drive, the fans were cheering so loud that the stadium was shaking. The biggest thing about Shea was I can't ever remember fans leaving before the game was over— like they would do once the Jets made the move to Giants Stadium. Maybe it was the traffic on the George Washington Bridge that scared everyone. The drive after a game from Shea wasn't bad, and all the players lived on Long Island. The drive from Giants Stadium was a different animal. Most of the players still lived on Long Island because our training facility was still in Hempstead at Hofstra University. That 60-mile drive after the game took at least three hours. Leon Hess had made the call, not the players and not the fans. Like it or not, Giants Stadium was the home of both the Jets and Giants.

Following the 1983 season, I was hoping to grant a wish to a special kid. It took the Marty Lyons Foundation almost six months to raise enough money for our first recipient, Stephen, to have his wish fulfilled. Stephen was 17 years old and was diagnosed with Lymphoma. His wish was to attend the Super Bowl in Tampa. The Jets allowed me to call a press conference, and with Stephen by my side, we launched the foundation. I had the total support of the organization from Mr. Hess, the owner, right down to my teammates, especially Kenny Schroy. Stephen was a strong young man. He was soft-spoken and brave enough to talk about his illness and being the first recipient of the foundation.

Unfortunately, Stephen passed away before the end of the '83 season and never got to the Super Bowl. I remember attending his wake, telling his father how sorry I was and how much I appreciated Stephen doing the press conference with me. His father leaned over and said to me very quietly, "Stephen was a great kid. He really wanted to do that press conference with you." Then he continued asking, "How long do you intend on doing this foundation?" I quickly answered that I hoped to do it my entire life. "Can I give you some advice?" He said. "Do the work of the foundation because you want to do it. Do it because it comes from the heart. Don't do it because you want to read about it in the newspaper. My son, Stephen, was strong, proud to see his picture in the newspapers the next day after the press conference, but for me when I went back to work the next day, I had co-workers walk right by me, not knowing what to say because they didn't know I had a child that was sick." I've never forgotten that conversation.

Lyons Life Lesson

The moments you enjoy the most are the good deeds that you do that no one knows about, the ones that warm the heart, and the ones that make you feel good from the inside out.

CHAPTER 7
The Middle Years

The 1984 season was going to have a completely different look. Personnel changes included a new starting quarterback in Kenny O'Brien. Plus we had two first-round draft picks that could help us build for the future. In the first round, the Jets took Russell Carter out of SMU and with the 15th pick they selected Ron Faurot out of Arkansas. Second-round picks were Jim Sweeney out of Pitt and Glenn Dennison, a tight end out of Miami, and the third-round pick was Kyle Clifton out of TCU. When you have two picks in the first round and then two more in the second, you can build a team if all the players can make the transition from college ball to the NFL. But Carter and Faurot ended up being complete whiffs. Cater played for a couple of years but never had a true impact on the defense. Faurot was a project that the Jets tried to transform into the next Ted Hendricks just because both of them were 6'7" in height. But the Jets never let Faurot develop into the player he could have been. The lack of these two first-round picks paying off hurt the Jets in the late '80s. The draft, though, did pay off with Sweeney and Clifton. They are two of the finest teammates that I had, and both worked hard in practice and made an impact for years to come with the New York Jets.

We once again had an up-and-down season in 1984, ending up at 7–9. Following every losing season, there had to be changes on the way. When you lose, it's not just the players who get released or fired. Out was our defensive coordinator Joe Gardi. He was one of those coaches who worked his way up the ranks. Gardi went from a high school coach to a college coach to a long career in the NFL. His biggest theme for the defense every day at practice and especially during the game was swarming to the ball. So I thought it would be pretty neat at the end of every preseason to have a swarm party for the team. Camp was over, the regular season was a week away, and players were reunited with their families. The party was at Eisenhower Park, and I invited everyone in the organization, including players, coaches, front-office personnel, everyone's family. We had a lot of fun at the party, and Mr. Hess, the owner of the team, would join in.

Gardi went right across the street on Hempstead Turnpike and coached Hofstra football. He did that from 1990 till 2005. He coached the Flying Dutchmen to a record of 119–62–2, and a lot of his guys went on to play in the NFL, including Jets wide receiver Wayne Cherbet.

After the 1984 season, team leader, running back, and special teams return man Bruce Harper retired. To this day, Harper remains a Jets fans favorite. Harper was an undersized player with a huge heart, was active in the community, and was a great teammate.

That year—like many others in the 1980s—I battled against a former Alabama star. New England Patriots offensive lineman and future Hall of Famer John Hannah was one of the toughest guys I had to line up against in the NFL. He was strong and low to the ground. New England always seemed to have our number. That offensive line was outstanding, starting with their center Pete Brock. Hannah and I had our battles, but I remember playing the Patriots one game where I whacked my hamstring and had to leave the game. My replacement was an undersized tackle by the name of Kenny Neil, who was a ball of energy. He went in the game for a few plays, and the official called unnecessary roughness on No. 73. That was Hannah's number. When was the last time you saw an offensive lineman called for unnecessary roughness? Neil came running over to the sideline. His helmet was twisted almost completely sideways, and he yelled, "That guy's trying to kill me." "Welcome to the NFL," I told him.

That year I also was named the NFL Man of the Year and presented the Miller Lite Man of the Year award, which was renamed later the Walter Payton Award. This was an honor not just for myself and my family, but also for all the children from the Marty Lyons Foundation. This award allowed people to hear their stories and identify with the pain the families endured after losing their children. Even through the award had my name of it, I still recognize it as the children's award.

When you come off back-to-back 7–9 seasons, the offseason feels even longer. Everywhere you go, longtime Jets fans wanted answers. I didn't have any. There were no miracle solutions, but one change that would pay off was the hiring of Bud Carson to be our new defensive coordinator. He was great with Xs and Os. His resume already included two Super Bowl rings he earned with the Pittsburgh Steelers during the 1970s. Carson had one rule. After an interception he wanted the quarterback on the ground. He always preached that a quarterback is a defender trying to make a tackle at that point. During practices he read the defense off a written script that matched up with the play that the scout team was running. So to get a little edge on Ted Banker, I learned how to sneak a peak and read upside down. Knowing the play was helpful, but getting the snap count was even easier. When we broke the huddle, the offense came to the line, and all you had to do was ask what the snap count was on. One of the offensive linemen would think it was one of their own and shout out two or one. So although Banker was holding, I also had an advantage. As many fights as we got into in practice, we probably had just as many beers together afterward.

It was during the 1984 season that I read an article about a young boy being set on fire by his father in a hotel over a custody battle. I couldn't believe that a father would have that much evil in his heart to do such a thing. I had the Jets public relations department reach out to the family and invited him to one of our Saturday practices. When he showed up with burns over 90 percent of his body, you could see grown men fighting back tears. That was a day that not only reminded us of how fortunate we are, but also what happiness you can bring to those in need.

After that disappointing year in 1984, the Jets redeemed themselves in the 1985 draft by selecting wide receiver Al Toon in the first round out of Wisconsin with their 10th overall pick. Toon had great speed, great hands, and was nothing but a professional from the first day he came to camp. He had a long career with the Jets, played in a couple of Pro

Bowls, and would later be voted in as part of the New York Jets Ring of Honor. Toon was a perfect teammate.

The real shocker came right before the first preseason game in 1985 when Joe Walton cut linebacker Greg Buttle in training camp. That move seemed personal to me. He deserved the same right that most players would get after a long career with one team. They either retired with class or were cut early enough to latch on with another team. But cutting Buttle before the first preseason game sent a message to everyone that no one was safe. After he was gone, we wondered who the team leader was going to be.

I was outside the locker room early in the season when Mr. Hess approached me. He asked how I was feeling and if I thought the team was ready for the season. He told me that Walton had asked him to say a few words to the team before the game. Mr. Hess then paused and said that the team didn't want to hear from him; they wanted to hear from me. "Sometimes you don't choose to be the leader. Sometimes people just choose to follow you," Hess said. "You're their leader."

Without Buttle the defensive unit looked for new leadership starting with Lance Mehl and Clifton. Carson's scheme was going to utilize an attack defense, and that's exactly what we did. He took Joe Klecko and moved him to a set position over the center shooting the A gap (the gap between the center and guard) almost on every play. Klecko utilized his speed and strength to get in the backfield, causing chaos for the opposing teams. Our defense was solid, and we were good enough to end the season 11–5. That was good but not good enough. The Miami Dolphins went 12–4 to win the division, and New England also went 11–5 that season to tie the Jets for second place in the AFC East.

With an 11–5 record, we played in the wild-card game against New England. During the regular season, we split the two-game series. All the players who were on the team in 1982 remembered how we lost to Miami three times in one season and we tried to prepare for New

England the best we could. Well, our best wasn't good enough that game, and we lost to New England 26–14. Another season ended with hopes of a Super Bowl dashed.

With the playoffs over for the Jets, housecleaning took place once again. This time it was Marvin Powell. The five-time Pro Bowl player was a leader on the field and in the locker room. He didn't get enough credit for developing Mark Gastineau into the player he was. Every day those two went at it full speed, and I believe that Powell made him a better player.

After the '85 season, my roommate and best friend with the Jets, Kenny Schroy, retired. He was not just an outstanding football player during his 10-year career, but he also was an outstanding person. What people didn't realize was the impact that Schroy had on and off the field. I witnessed both. On the field he was the starting strong safety, which meant that he had to come up a lot in run support and also had to protect

I remain great friends with Kenny Schroy, my former roommate and teammate who retired after the 1985 season.

the middle of the field on pass coverage. Schroy also was responsible for making all the secondary calls.

He and I were roommates on the road for five years until the room got too cold for him, and the fog rolled in. Yes, the fog rolled in. We were getting ready to play the Cleveland Browns late in the season, and I had a routine the night before the game that I always followed. I would take a hot shower and then turn the shower from hot to cold, ending the shower in almost a deep freeze. No matter where we were playing, I would drop the room temperature to 60 degrees and jump in bed wearing a pair of boxers. Meanwhile, Schroy wore a sweatsuit and double blanket. That night I just couldn't get settled in, couldn't get comfortable. I felt hot, so I opened the window to let the cold Cleveland air into the room. The only problem was when we woke up the fog covered the room to the point I couldn't see Schroy or the other side of the room. He got up, looked at me, and politely said, "That's it. We're done being roommates. I can't take it any longer."

Off the field he was involved in helping me start The Marty Lyons Foundation. Even before the foundation was started, Schroy made a lot of visits to hospitals with me. When I started the foundation in 1982, he was really a co-founder. Without his support and dedication, I couldn't have done it by myself. For 35 years he has served on the foundation's board. He was very instrumental in the growth of the foundation and our annual Christmas party. He knew why we were doing the work and that our mission was bigger than the both of us.

You know you have someone special in your life when they become Uncle Kenny to your children, and you become Uncle Marty to his children also. That's what the game of football does. It brings people together.

His career in football started as a running back in Quakertown, Pennsylvania. He wasn't just good; he was great. He remains the only player in Quakertown High School history to have his number retired. But in 1986 his No. 48 would be worn by another Jets player.

Schroy taught me a lot. He influenced me into becoming the person I am today. He lived his life with one simple rule: tell people the truth. I realized that it's not always about getting the credit one deserves. It's about knowing who you are and knowing in the end that results are what matters. I thank Schroy for his friendship, love, and dedication to me, my family, and the children of the Marty Lyons Foundation.

Lyons Life Lesson

To be the best, you have to be willing to face the best. You may not win the fight all the time, but picking yourself up off the ground and fighting again builds character and self-esteem.

CHAPTER 8
Wesley Walker, Mark Gastineau, and the Wild-Card

The 1986 season started out great for the Jets organization, fans, and the players. After beginning the season 1–1, we won nine straight games. The biggest game came in Week Three against the Miami Dolphins at Giants Stadium. Dan Marino was unstoppable; he threw for six touchdowns and 448 yards in the shootout. No matter what defense we were in, we couldn't stop him. But they couldn't stop Kenny O'Brien and Wesley Walker. O'Brien threw for 479 yards and four touchdowns. It was almost like watching arena football because of all the scoring. Whoever stopped the opposing team one time might just win the game. I still run into fans today who claim that was the best game they ever saw the Jets play. I quickly remind them that it wasn't if you were on the defensive side that day. Walker, who had four touchdown catches, had a terrific game.

Walker was a one-of-a kind player and person. Blinded in one eye since birth, he became one of the most effective wide receivers in the NFL. He was the best locker room teammate you could ask for and always had your back. I remember taking him to different golf tournaments. On one occasion he forgot his golf clubs, so we went into the pro shop and asked for a set of rentals. The guy behind the courter asked if he wanted a right-handed or left-handed set. Walker quickly answered, "It doesn't matter. I'm not that good."

When it came to a golf tournament with him, there was always a story that would make you laugh. One time we went to an outing, and he blew out the side of his golf shoe. He went into the pro shop to buy a new pair. When he came out, he looked like Daffy Duck walking in a pair of size 13 shoes. I walked over and said, "Dude, what's with the shoes?"

He laughed. "The guy in the pro shop said that the shoes I was wearing were too tight on my feet, and that's what caused me to blow out the side, so I bought bigger shoes."

As I laughed, I said, "Wesley, those are size 13. You only wear a size 10."

When I suffered a stroke in the summer of 2017, I was in a hospital getting wheeled over for a brain MRI at 8:00 AM in the morning. As I was going down the hallway, a door opened, and Walker walked out. Our eyes made contact, and then Walker spoke first, "Dude, what are you doing here?"

As I explained my situation, tears came from both of our eyes. He hugged me, told me he loved me, and that he would check on me later. Walker had actually been there that morning to take in an older friend for a check-up because she couldn't drive. He then got the word out about me that morning to former teammates, and the calls kept coming in with concerns about my health. Walker is one of a kind, the type of person everyone should have as a friend.

Later that year in October we played the Buffalo Bills. Jim Kelly was the quarterback and was tougher than nails. Kelly was so tough that he could have played any position on the field,. During the week our beat reporter told us that Kelly made a statement that he wasn't worried about the Jets pass rush because we were pretty much over the hill. He might have been right, but we still had a game to play. Early in the game, I hit Kelly as he was going out of bounds with the ball. Of course, Kelly didn't like it so he got up and threw the ball at me. I went after him and proceeded to get my ass kicked because I was on their sideline.

As the game went into the second quarter, Kelly rolled out to throw a pass. I hit him as he was throwing the ball and ended up on top of him. Kelly quickly changed from a quarterback to a linebacker and told me to get the fuck off him. Well, I was on top and told him to go fuck himself and I punched him about 10 times. As Kelly and I were shaking hands, the call came from the official Ben Dreith, who said, "Personal foul—No. 99 [he mistakenly said Mark Gastineau's number] was giving the quarterback the business." Dreith even made the gesture of holding someone in a headlock and pumping his fist up and down like he was punching someone. To this day that must be one of the funniest NFL calls ever.

Later in the season, Jimmy the Greek on CBS said we wouldn't win any of our last five games. *Who did he think he was? We would lose five straight games after winning nine in a row?* Well, it turns out we were outscored 183–61. We gave up 45 points or more in three of the last five games, and Jimmy the Greek was right. We lost our last five games. During the last five weeks, we had so many injuries that it was like a revolving door at the Jets complex. I was playing in a double shoulder harness to keep both shoulders from popping out. Joe Klecko was hurt, and O'Brien was hurt, but we had no one to blame for our poor performance except ourselves. Injuries are part of the game. You learn how to win in the NFL playing through injuries. And no one is going to feel sorry for you in the NFL. It's a long season. One play you're a backup player, and the next play you're a starter.

Because we played so well from Week Three to Week 11, we made the playoffs and once again played in the wild-card game. It's so important to get that first-round bye in the playoffs. You get to heal a little and most likely you're going to get a home game. If only we won one or two of those last five games, maybe things would have been different. But we had a chance to forget about that five-game losing streak if we could just win our opener against the Kansas City Chiefs.

Our team was really banged up, starting with O'Brien. He was as tough as could be, but would he be ready? Would Joe Walton make a change at that position? Nobody really knew until midway through the week when Walton made the announcement that backup quarterback Pat Ryan would start the game. Everyone loved Ryan. If you couldn't have Klecko in the foxhole with you, you wanted Ryan. He didn't have the arm strength that O'Brien had, but Ryan was a fighter who outlasted the likes of Richard Todd and Matt Robinson for a reason. He knew his role with the team, didn't have an ego about being a backup, and knew how to control the huddle and locker room. Just maybe after losing five in row, Ryan would be that spark we needed.

The game was in Giants Stadium. It was cold and windy. We knew as a defense we had to play better. Hell, you couldn't have played any worse then we did the last five games. We couldn't have asked the offense to play any better. They scored 35 points. Ryan was outstanding, completing 69 percent of his passes and throwing for three touchdowns. The offensive line did a great job blocking for Freeman McNeil as he ran for more than 100 yards and had two touchdowns. Bud Carson had the defense playing well. We pinned our ears back and flew around the ball for the entire 60 minutes. We gave up 15 points and held the Chiefs to a season low 241 total yards. We got a nice payday for winning—$6,000 per man—but more importantly, we moved on to the divisional game at the Cleveland Browns the following week.

We didn't have much time to heal. I already knew that I was scheduled for shoulder surgery as soon as the season was over. I'd have my right shoulder done, and then a month later, my left shoulder would be done. I didn't practice at all during the week. And when gameday arrived, I already knew the procedure: injections before the game, more at halftime, and again at the end of the game. Let me make this perfectly clear: the Jets doctor and trainers did not force me to take any of the injections. But if I wanted to play, it was the only way.

We had a question at starting quarterback. Was it O'Brien or Ryan? It really didn't matter to us. They were both winners. Both ended up playing, but Ryan started the game. Regardless, we lost 23–20 in double overtime, even though we had a 10-point lead with four minutes to go in the fourth quarter. It was a very disappointing way to end the season.

Winning nine games in a row didn't matter anymore. It was back to another long offseason, and for me that meant two trips to Lenox Hill Hospital to get my shoulders fixed. Both of my shoulder surgeries went well. I had one the best doctors, Frank Mendoza, do both. My goal now was rehab and trying my best to get back for the start of the 1987 season.

We should have never lost to the Browns. We just didn't play for a full 60 minutes. We didn't lose it on one play. Everyone points to Gastineau's late hit on Bernie Kosar on a second and 24, but that play just gave the Browns an extra chance. The entire team could have done a better job, and that included the coaching staff. With a 10-point lead in the fourth quarter, you have to put the opposing team away. We didn't. Cleveland had 33 first downs, and we had only 14. The defense played well for 56 minutes and forgot about the other four minutes. The offensive line gave up nine sacks, and the defense allowed Kosar to throw for more than 480 yards.

Gastineau's play didn't cost us the game. As a defensive player, though, you always have to know the referee. In this case in was Dreith. It seemed like his No. 1 rule was don't sneeze on the quarterback, and if you did, he threw a flag. Flag or no flag, we lost the game as a team.

As anyone could tell you, Gastineau and I weren't close as teammates. I respected him as a player and supported him, but we didn't hang out or run in the same social circle. But on March 7, 2019, I got a strange call from Gastineau telling me he had stage-four colon cancer. He called needing help and was reaching out to me for guidance and support. As I reflected on our relationship, there are things we could have done differently both on and off the field. For all of us, there are things that we have done in our past to hurt people or disrespect people, but we can't live in the past. We must find a way to forgive, give people a second chance, maybe even a third or fourth chance. Don't point the finger at someone else without pointing at yourself.

My wife, Christine, always says, "Things happen for a reason." The day after Gastineau called was the anniversary of my father, Leo, passing away 37 years before. It was a day to celebrate his life and his impact as a father and husband. Leo wasn't always right, but he set the foundation for my brothers and sisters to build on. That's the strange thing about life. There will always be a day and there will always be an event that will remind us of the loved ones who have passed away. Two days after grieving for my father, I spent the morning at the cemetery to pay respect to Keith, the little boy for whom I started the Marty Lyons Foundation. He would've have been 44 years old in 2020. He probably would have had a family of his own, but God had other plans for him. As I stood in the rain, it helped hide the tears running down my face. The pain was real. I was the only person in the whole cemetery and spent it reflecting on a friendship that made me a better person. In the end Keith made an impact on so many lives, and all the children from the foundation are a direct reflection of my love for my dad and Keith.

Lyons Life Lesson

Time is more valuable than money. You can always make more money, but you can't make more time. Value the time you have with family and friends, create memories, share laughter, and smile at one another.

CHAPTER 9
The Strike

The 1987 season started with a cloud over the players' heads. There was the possibility of another players' strike, and to make matters worse, the owners had voted to bring in replacement players to play the games. As a league we were not a strong union. We were divided by opinions and needs. If we were going to strike, the union's plans were to strike in the middle of the season when the television contracts were taking place and the stadium was full of fans to call the bluff of the owners and their replacement players. That was not a smart move. You can't call the bluff of billionaires. Owning an NFL team is a hobby for these owners. They already made their money elsewhere.

Meanwhile, I was getting ready to leave Demopolis, Alabama, where I had a farm with my family when my wife, Kelley, told me she was not coming up for the season. She and my son, Rocky, were staying back in Alabama. The day before I was leaving, she informed me of this. I knew my marriage was being held together with strings, and they had just gotten cut. I couldn't even fight her decision. She had waited until the last moment to tell me. Only time would tell if our marriage would last.

We won our first two games and then we walked out. Well, some of us did. The players were divided. Replacement players started to come in because the owners weren't bluffing. They were going to play these games. Week Three of the NFL schedule was canceled, and then replacement players started playing in Week Four and would play until the strike was over.

A few of us gave the union a check or two and crossed the picket line after the Week Four game. I believed in the cause, but someone was there trying to take my job along with my paycheck. I remember we were scheduled to play the Colts in Week Five in Indianapolis. We had to sneak into the Hoosier Dome with a police escort. Joe Walton approached me and asked if I could say something to the team. *Really, Joe?* I got to the stadium early, had a couple cups of coffee, and went to the field. To my surprise the replacements for the Jets were already there warming up. I remember one of the guys was trying a 50-yard field goal. Yep, he was warming up out of the box with 50-yard field goals! It was the funniest sight you would ever wanted to see. His attempts went left short, right short, right short, short, and I could go on and on because he never made a single kick. I ended up waving the kid over and told him to try kicking extra points. He said thanks and went back to the field with the same results.

When I returned to the locker room, the replacement players were getting taped and dressed. Players pounded on each others' shoulders pads and yelled and screamed like they hadn't played football since high school, and that was probably the case for some. I looked over to see one of the linebackers walking around with his thigh pads on backward. He had the left one in the right pocket and vice versa. If you know anything about thigh pads, there's a high side, and there's a low side. The low sides go toward the inside of your thigh, so you don't pinch your testicles. I'm like, *Really, dude, come on.* So I went up to him, explained that he had to switch the right pad with the left. "Thanks, man," he said. "I knew something was wrong."

What was wrong was that these players shouldn't have been in uniform representing the NFL, but the owners were proving a point. With or without the normal players, games would be played and they would be counted in the end. That day we lost to the Colts 6–0. It was funny but also pathetic.

The strike ended after three replacement games. When the entire team came in, the locker room was divided once again. Players were pissed off that some of us crossed the picket line and pissed off that some of the replacement players stayed around as part of the team. From name-calling to spitting on players, what I witnessed during that strike was unbelievable. Calling the replacement players "scabs" was totally disrespectful. All these replacement players wanted was an opportunity to play a game they loved, and we "the so-called real NFL players" under-estimated the power of the ownership and overestimated the power of the union.

On *Monday Night Football* on December 7, 1987 my life would change. I was involved in a play that ended the career of my good friend, Dwight Stephenson, who was a member of the Miami Dolphins. He and I were teammates at the University of Alabama and were part of the team that won a national championship in 1978. To this day I still relive that play against the Dolphins repeatedly, wishing the results would have been different.

I was stunting in the A gap between the center and the guard, when I looked up to see Dolphins quarterback Dan Marino throw a quick hitch to his wide receiver. I saw our corner jump the pass and intercept the ball. My next reaction was to block a Dolphins player. Out of the corner of my eye, I saw someone running, and when he turned completely, I hit him in the front, sending him to the ground. I heard the player yell as he hit the ground and looked down to see Stephenson holding his knee. He never saw me coming, and now he and I had to pay the price.

As the doctor and trainers were working on Stephenson, I took a knee and prayed. I was getting cussed at by every player and coach from the Dolphins staff, but I didn't leave the field until Stephenson did. Hell, I was getting yelled at by my own coaches to get off the field. When I made it to the sideline, the defensive line coach Ray Callahan took me out of the game. He was worried about the Dolphins' retaliation on me.

When I came in the league in 1979, the best center was Mike Webster of the Pittsburgh Steelers. Stephenson came into the league in 1980, and it didn't take long for him to assume that title as the best at his position. Now he was being taken off in a cart with his future unknown.

I quickly got to the locker room, showered, and headed over to the Dolphins locker room. I knew I was not going to be welcome in there, but still I had to see Stephenson and apologize for what happened. It was an accident that I would have to live with forever. Walking back to the trainers' room, the locker room was quiet. They beat us that night 37–28, but their big concern was the health of Stephenson. He was sitting there with his knee packed in ice. I expressed how sorry I was, and Stephenson told me it wasn't my fault and that it was part of the game. Even hearing his words didn't help the emptiness I had in my stomach. If only I had turned the other way and looked for a block on my right. It didn't matter. The damage was done.

As I was walking out of the locker room, I ran into Dolphins head coach Don Shula. He asked me what I was doing in his locker room. When I replied I was here to talk to Stephenson, he went into a fit. He took me into the Dolphins equipment room. I don't remember how I got up against the wall, but there I was with Coach Shula in my face. He went off. I was called every name in the book and I never forgot the last thing he said to me, "I hope you can live with yourself."Then he turned and walked out. The Dolphins equipment manager Bobby Monica, who witnessed the whole thing, came over to me and said, "You didn't deserve that." Maybe Monica was right, but I had so much respect for Coach Shula. He just lost the best lineman on his team. Either way that play changed my life and unfortunately also changed Stephenson's.

That one play haunted me all the way back to New York, as I relived it over and over. *What could I have done different? Would that one play define my entire career?* As soon as we landed and got back to the Jets complex, I watched the films. Yes, it was just like I remembered it. Stephenson never saw me coming and he fell in an awful position. To this day I regret the results of that block. Coach Shula was right. I would have to live with that play the rest of my life.

Later that year on October 30, Kelley was in a terrible car accident with Rocky when she flipped the truck she was driving, slid across the highway, and went down an embankment about 30 feet. Only by the

I still feel awful about Dwight Stephenson's knee injury. But my former Alabama teammate and I remain friends.

grace of God did they both survive. Rocky pushed his mother up the hill and waved down a car to take them both to the hospital.

Heading into the month of December, we were 6–5 and still had a chance to make the playoffs. All we had to do was to win in the month of December. To make it to the playoffs, you must start the season off fast, winning in the month of September, and finish strong in the month of December, something the Jets have always had problems doing. This December was the same story. We lost our final four games.

So, as any good teammates would do, we had a going-away party on the Friday night before we played the New England Patriots. Walton was also feeling the pressure of a split locker room and the pressure to win. His speeches to the team during the week started with the statement: "You guys are stealing from the club. Some of you should back up to the pay window to get your checks." If Walton thought this was a way to motivate the team, he was dead wrong. Instead it felt disrespectful. You don't motivate a team that way. We all felt the pressure to win.

Saturday night before the New England game, Walton once again gave us his pep talk about the game, how we could prove that we were football players. All that bullshit didn't motivate us nor was it going to help us feel better about ourselves. In the NFL coaches can only do so much to get the team ready to play; the rest is on the players. That next day it wasn't Walton's speech that cost us the game. It was the terrible way we played. We lost 42–20. We didn't play as a team, for each other, or certainly for Coach Walton.

The shit was going to hit the fan Monday morning. Walton called a team meeting with the players, and all the assistant coaches were excused from the meeting. Walton came into the meeting, chewing his cigar with fire in his eyes. He started the meeting, saying how disappointed he was in our performance in New England. He didn't have to tell us that. We knew it and also felt it. He then complimented himself, saying he thought he gave the best pregame speech Saturday night, and it fell on deaf ears. Then he dropped the unexpected bomb. "I understand that you guys had a team party on Friday night," he said.

That cigar Walton was chewing got smaller and smaller as he continued. "So a team party two nights before a game?" He said before calling out players to see if they were there. "Al Toon, were you at the party?"

"No sir," Toon replied.

"Great team party when you don't have one of you best teammates there. Jo Jo Townsell, were you there?"

"No sir," Townsell replied.

You could feel the rage in Walton's voice when he called the next name out. "Marty Lyons, were you at the party?"

All the eyes in the meeting turned to me. "Yes sir, I was there."

If it wasn't for the tension in the room, it would have been filled with laughter as Walton almost choked on his cigar. I really don't remember how the mood of the meeting shifted back to Walton's speech on Saturday night, but Rocky Klever got up and told Walton what he thought about the speech. Klever got right to the point. "Joe, I thought it sucked."

With that statement Klever had just signed a one-way ticket out of the organization. Everyone in the room that day knew it. Then the heavyweight fight we were all waiting for was about to happen: Joe Klecko vs. Joe Walton. Those two went after each other like there was no tomorrow. Klecko did what he had always done since the first day I met him back in 1979. He defended his teammates.

The '87 season was over. After the speeches and physicals were completed, good-byes were said, and it meant another long offseason for the players, coaches, and fans. I was driving back to my farm in Alabama down the New Jersey Turnpike when breaking news came across the radio. In a surprise move, the Jets had released Klecko and Joe Fields less than 24 hours after losing their final game of the 1987 season to the New York Giants. Wow, it didn't take long for Walton to put the hammer down.

The only good news about 1987 was that I opened the third chapter of the Marty Lyons Foundation. With the help of so many volunteers and donors, the foundation was now operating in New York, New Jersey, and Florida.

One of our first wishes from Florida was from a two-and-a-half-year-old boy for a camcorder. It's something that you and I would take for granted, but the family wanted something to capture their son's attention. We ended up sending the camcorder to them on a Monday. On Tuesday they had a surprise birthday party for their son, even though it wasn't his birthday. On Wednesday their child died. On Friday of that week I talked to the father and expressed how sorry I was, and his comment still reminds me today of why we do the work we do. "If it wasn't for you, your foundation, and all of the people that believe in your cause, we wouldn't have any memories to hold on to," he said. "Thank you for doing what you do."

The 1987 season was over, but the outside world was speaking louder, reminding me that there were more important things to achieve than trophies for the game of football.

Lyons Life Lesson

Sometime in life you might say something or do something where saying I'm sorry just isn't enough.

God has given each one of us a platform. Use it for others before you use it for yourself. Touch as many people as you can and change their lives while changing your own.

Life is fragile; live for today. That lesson was hammered home when I found out Johnny "Lam" Jones lost his battle to cancer in March of 2019. The news of Lam passing was also a reminder to all of us that football—while it was our livelihood, a career for which God given us the tools to pursue—didn't last forever for anyone of us, but our friendships did.

CHAPTER 10
"Joe Must Go"

With Joe Klecko gone and Joe Fields gone, the team had to find new leaders in the locker room as well as fill the void on the defensive and offensive line in 1988. The 1988 draft looked very promising, as the Jets took Dave Cadigan with the eighth overall pick in the first round. A big-bodied guy out of USC, Cadigan ended up playing seven years with the Jets but never fully reached his potential. Players that were a surprise from that draft were Erik McMillan, James Hasty, and Paul Frase, and all three had an impact on our 1988 season.

McMillan was the type of player every team wanted and needed. He was a hard hitter, a student of the game, and also a quality person. If your daughter brought a guy like McMillan home, you would give your blessing. There are only two celebrities—Joe Namath and McMillan—who I have flown in for a Marty Lyons Foundation golf outing. That should tell you how I feel about McMillan.

The players were in place, but the heat was on the entire coaching staff to win. The Jets fans were frustrated and they let us know every time we lost at home. The "Joe Must Go" signs were out, the boo birds were singing, and life as a New York Jets player was tough. Joe Walton always made it seem like the attack was just on him. He came into meetings, telling the team how hard it was for him to go into a deli to get a sandwich or how his son was getting harassed in school. I felt like telling him, "No shit, we all have that same experience with our families."

Hell, I was doing some promotional work with Honda at the time, and the car company would give me a free car every 10,000 miles. All I had to do was allow them to put a license plate with JETS 93 on the car. Easy enough, right? I can't tell you how many one finger waves I got or how many times someone pulled up alongside of me and rolled down their window just to yell, "You suck!" Without a doubt we were all in the same boat. The question was how many of us would survive the season.

In Week Six we played the Cincinnati Bengals on the road. The night before the game, I did my same routine: took a hot shower, took a cold shower, got the room as cold as possible, and went to bed. That night's sleep was like no other I ever had. I saw the game unfolding right in front of my eyes. I sacked the quarterback, made tackles all over the field, recovered a fumble, had another sack. I woke up with the bed being torn apart in a cold sweat.

The dream was so real that I had to tell someone about it the next morning at the pregame meal. So I told Kyle Clifton and Jim Sweeney. Those guys couldn't stop laughing, but they wanted to know if we won. I told them I didn't know because I woke up, which brought another round of belly laughs. Well, that afternoon I probably had one of my best games as a pro. I had three sacks, a fumble recovery, and 13 tackles. I can't tell you how many times I tried to have another dream like that, but it did prove to me the power of the mind. But maybe I woke up too early because we ended up losing the game 36–19.

Midway through the 1988 season, Mark Gastineau decided that he was going to retire from football to spend time with his fiancée Brigitte Nielsen who was sick. Gastineau didn't tell any of his teammates. He just left. I can respect that Gastineau left for personal reasons. Looking back some 30 years, I think if he had decided to take a couple of weeks off to deal with the health issues, that would have sat better with a lot of the guys, but he choose to retire.

I had to take two weeks away from the team in 1987 when my family was in a terrible car accident, and the organization completely understood. I truly believe the Jets would have done the same for Gastineau as he dealt with his situation. When he retired in 1988, he still had a lot of football left in his body. He could still get to the quarterback and he still could help any team in the NFL. But the way he exited the Jets left a sour taste in everyone's mouth and closed the door on any possible return to the NFL. It really was a sad ending for a tremendous player.

One of the weirder stories of that 1988 season happened in training camp that year. We had a scrimmage with the Washington Redskins in

Pennsylvania on a Saturday afternoon at Lafayette College. We were getting ready to do an 11-on-11 team when a white limo pulled behind the Jets bench on the track. The driver got out and opened the back door, and out came Nielsen dressed from top to bottom in all white. To this day the question has never been answered: with all the security the Jets had and the college had, how could they let that limo on the field?

We were 7–7–1 going into the last game against the New York Giants. The Giants were 10–5 and in the hunt to make it into the play-offs. Our defensive coordinator, Bud Carson, never pulled any punches. He always told us the truth. Carson's pregame speech was simple and to the point. He said, "I don't know my future here. I may be fired after the game, and if you SOBs don't play hard, I'm going to take a few of you with me." It was plain, simple, and truthful.

We had only the pride and dignity—that which wasn't stripped from us by our own head coach—to play for. They say you win the game up front, and that was exactly what we did. We sacked Phil Simms eight times and only allowed two sacks by the Giants. But we did have a hard time stopping the run, as the Giants rushed for almost 200 yards. That game might have been the only game that we played as a team and won as a team. In seven games we allowed more than 28 points and we only scored 28 points or more in five games. But we beat the Giants 27–21 in our final game, and the Giants fell to 10–6, which meant their season was over without a playoff berth too.

The next day was the same as any season-ending year. We had one last meeting, physicals, and a final good-bye to teammates. Life in the NFL meant no team rosters would ever be the same year to year. To my surprise Walton wanted to have a one-on-one meeting with me before I left and headed to Alabama for the offseason. The meeting didn't start off nor end well. Walton asked me what player in the locker room didn't believe in him and his coaching methods. I just shook my head and didn't give any answer. *Did he really think I was going to rat out my teammates?*

Then he asked me a final question: "Do you want to be on this team next year?"

My immediate answer was: "yes sir."

Then he quickly went back to the first question. "Then tell me what players I should get rid of," he said.

I had no answer. Walton told me to think about it and that we would meet again at the end of January.

Looking back on it, maybe Walton thought of me as a leader and he wanted my opinion on the team, or maybe he thought I would start screaming out names. I don't know, but what I did know was the four walls of the Jets complex were getting squeezed together and I was in the middle of them.

Life off the field was 100 percent geared toward my foundation. I tried to move on from my divorce that was finalized in May. Visiting the hospitals and meeting the kids was my platform, my way of escaping from the world of football. When you went to visit the kids in the hospitals, they didn't care how many games you won that year. They felt important. I sat there in the playroom and drew pictures with them, laughed with them, and tried my best to show the families the support they needed to get them through a difficult time. Kids walked around with IV poles and were bald from all the chemotherapy treatments. I don't remember seeing both parents by the bedside. Normally, it was their mother, who was sleeping in the chair right next to the bed. I always left the hospital feeling better about myself than when I went in. I left with more friends and looked at life a lot different. Boy, was I blessed.

I once got into a conversation with a mother of four about religion. I asked her how often she prayed. To my surprise, she answered that she hadn't prayed in 30 years. "Really," I said. "Why so long?"

She went on to tell me that when she was a little girl, her mother got diagnosed with cancer, and everyone told her that if she prayed to God, everything would be okay. She prayed every night for months, and her mother still passed away, God didn't answer any of her prayers. I went on to tell her that—as difficult as it is come to terms with—it was God's way of trying to get her to find her path in life. I explained to her that I also had to find my path in 1982 when God took two of my loved ones in a matter of two days.

After the NFL draft the following year, I realized my stay with the Jets was closing in. The Jets drafted Jeff Lageman in the first round, Dennis Byrd in the second round, Ron Stallworth in the fourth round, and Marvin Washington in the sixth round. They were all defensive linemen. Lageman was listed as an outside linebacker but he put his hand in the dirt and played defensive end in all passing situations. We already had Gerald Nichols, Paul Frase, and Scott Mersereau. It was just a matter of time before the youth of the team would catch up to me, and my number would be called.

That draft was special for me. I got to witness one of the best choices for the Jets. Byrd developed into an NFL star. Hungry to play and hungry to take my position, Byrd was exciting. I was in my 11th year. I would help Byrd in his development, but first I was going to mess with him. I created an imaginary team, a minor league team called the Bridgeport Jets, where players went that weren't ready for the NFL. Players there played on a 10-game schedule, traveled on buses to and from games, and received only a couple hundreds of dollars per game. To make Byrd believe that the Bridgeport Jets really existed, I had fake stat sheets made up. Best of all, I had players in the locker room come by my locker when Byrd was close by and ask me a simple question like, "Hey Marty, what is it like playing for the Bridgeport Jets?"

I would make up an answer, knowing that Byrd was listening. Byrd then asked about the team. So I knew I had him hooked and that he had taken the bait. From that day forward, Byrd worked harder than I ever saw a player work. After practice he would ask the same question,

"Do you think I'll make the team, or do you think I'll get shipped to Bridgeport?"

I would tell him Bridgeport wasn't that bad. Even though you didn't get your NFL contract, you'd get a chance to develop. I even took it to the limit when I had a beat reporter ask him what he thought about playing one year with the minor league team. Instead of going into a shell, Byrd kept working harder. It wasn't until the third preseason game when he had two sacks and he was celebrating that I told him the truth: there was no minor league team. Welcome to the NFL.

Byrd was unique. He was a man of God. He wore his religion on his sleeve, but he never pushed his beliefs on any of us. We respected him and appreciated him as a teammate and friend. We developed a personal friendship his rookie season, one that lasted a lifetime. Byrd had one bad habit. Anytime he went to make a tackle, he ducked his head and led with the crown of the helmet. Greg Robinson, the defensive line coach, pointed it out repeatedly to Byrd and tried his best to solve a habit that should have been corrected in peewee, high school, or college football—not in the NFL.

When the season started, it didn't take the Jets fans too long to let the players and the coaches know what they thought of our performance every Sunday. The boos were loud, and planes with signs that said "Joe Must Go" flew all over the stadium. "The Joe Must Go" chants got louder and louder with every home game we played. If we didn't turn this thing around, we'd all be gone at the end of the season.

But the year was nothing short of ugly. We went 4–12. Walton was fired. I only played in 10 games that season due to a knee injury so my future was up in the air. When the day came for me to retire, I already had decided that I would make my home in New York. I wanted to get into coaching when it was over. With the growth of my foundation, how could I just pick up and go elsewhere?

Walton moved on to become a great college coach at Robert Morris University in Moon Township, Pennsylvania. He was so good at the collegiate level that they built a stadium on campus and named it after him. We all learned a lot over Walton's seven years with the Jets, but we only went to the playoffs twice and were always trying to rebuild. For me to say it was all on Walton and the way he coached would be unfair to him. The players themselves must be accountable, and as one of them, I take responsibility for not playing better. With losing comes change, and change was coming in the form of an entirely new staff.

Lyons Life Lesson

Before you try to accomplish anything, visualize yourself accomplishing the task first. The mind is the most powerful part of the body.

Finding your path in life isn't always easy. You'll be challenged, and the biggest obstacle to ever overcome is a death of a love one. It will challenge you to your core. All you need to do is have faith that God has a plan for you. It's not your plan. It is his. That plan will never be what you think it should be until you fully allow God to have ownership of your life.

CHAPTER 11
Hanging It Up

The Jets announced their new head coach would be Bruce Coslet. The previous season he was the offensive coordinator for the Cincinnati Bengals. Coslet put together a great staff on paper, but the big question was could we win. I look back and realize that Coslet was in a no-win situation in 1990. Every assistant coach wants to be a head coach of his own team one day, but that team needs to develop and have some stability at the top, something the Jets were still trying to find or develop. What made the pressure even greater was the team across the river. The New York Giants were not only winning, but they were also winning Super Bowls.

It looked like the Jets had a promising draft, taking Blair Thomas out of Penn State in the first round and drafting wide receiver Reggie Rembert out of West Virginia. Unfortunately, both players couldn't make the transition from outstanding collegiate player to outstanding NFL player. Later in that draft, the Jets did hit on two offensive lineman, Dwayne White and Roger Duffy, who both had long careers in the NFL.

Pete Carroll was our defensive coordinator. After being in the league since 1984 as a position coach, he was given a chance to bring his own style of defense to the Jets. Carroll also brought in Monte Kiffin to coach the linebackers and Greg Robinson to coach the defensive line. Robinson was a 38-year-old coach from UCLA, and at that time, I was 33.

Robinson and I didn't start out on the same page from Day One. I was in the weight room lifting by myself when he came over and introduced himself. He asked me if we could go outside and hit one of the blocking sleds when I was done lifting. When we got outside, I did a few drills with him. After watching me he asked how many years I had been in the NFL. When I told him 12, he remarked that he was in disbelief that I still didn't know how to properly hit a sled. He wanted me to watch some college film with him so I could see how to do it correctly. I put my foot in my mouth when I said, "I'm not watching any fucking college film." It was not the right answer, and once training camp started in a few months, I would pay dearly for it.

Robinson was just what the young defensive line needed, but he was not what I needed. He was go, go, go. I was like, *Come on. What about a break here?* He was doing all those drills like the monkey roll, which I hadn't done in years. I thought the guy was trying to kill me. But Robinson was perfect for the young players. He could mold them into the type of players he wanted them to be. But my body just didn't respond like it did when I was their age.

In our fourth preseason game, which was against the Giants, I went to make a tackle and felt my right arm go numb. When I went back to the huddle, I had this numbness in my fingers. One play later I looked at my right arm and saw that my bicep had snapped and rolled up into my shoulder. I ran off the field, saw the team doctors, and they confirmed that I tore my bicep and would need surgery the next day. My season was over before it even started. Prior to getting hurt, I knew for the first time in my career that I would be playing in a backup roll to Dennis Byrd, but that was okay because my ego wasn't that big about being a starter at this point in my career. I just wanted to play. And to honest with you, I knew that Byrd would give the Jets a better chance of winning. Byrd was going to be a special player for the Jets.

The thing about being injured is you don't feel as if you're part of the team. You're not included in team meetings. You don't go out to practice and you don't go to away games. The bottom line is you're just there. I get it. I was invisible. The team had to move on. It was a long season for me as I had to rehab on my own and try to get ready for hopefully another swing at the plate for the 1991 season. As for the Jets, it was another year of missing the playoffs with a 6–10 record.

In February of 1991 with my rehab completed, I got called to the office of general manager Dick Steinberg, who was sitting there with Coslet. Steinberg spoke first and complimented me about how good I looked. Then he dropped the bomb. "We're moving in a different direction. We have to get younger, and you're not in our plans," he said. "So you can either retire with class, or we're going to cut you tomorrow."

Wow. Cut and dry, it was over. I've seen it happen to so many of my teammates in the past and I wasn't any different. The only response I could muster was to ask how long I had to make my decision. "One day," Steinberg said.

I cleaned out my locker and went home to think about what would be best for me and my family. I decided that I came in with class in 1979 and would leave with class in 1991, so I called Steinberg the next morning and asked him to call a press conference for the following Monday.

On Monday I met Steinberg in his office and thanked him for the opportunity to retire with class and calling a press conference for me. Steinberg asked me a funny question that morning. He said, "Do you know what you're going to say this morning?"

When I asked what he was talking about, he said, "We want this to look good for the both of us." *Really, Steinberg, did you really just say that? The day I'm going to announce my retirement, you're worried about how it looks for you.* I've always respected the Jets organization and I was proud that they gave me the two options. They showed me respect; they could've just cut me like they did to Joe Klecko, Greg Buttle, and many, many more.

I remember standing in front of beat writers, saying, "I was at a point in my career where I had too much respect for Mr. Hess, the fans, and my teammates to wear a different color jersey, and for that reason and that reason only I was retiring." I kept it short and to the point. The reality of the whole situation was my mind wanted to play, but my body said no. I went to bed one day young and woke up the next old. I was finished. I just had to accept it.

A couple of weeks later, I went to thank Mr. Hess in New York City. From the choice that Steinberg gave me to my retirement announcement a couple of weeks later, I told him the entire story. To my surprise Mr. Hess looked over to the phone and said he could pick it up and have my job back tomorrow. I assured him that was not the reason for my visit. I really wanted to thank him for everything he did for my family and me. Mr. Hess was a kind person that I greatly respected, and at the end of my career, I considered him a friend. Football was over, but life would go on.

Now it was time to move on to a second career or maybe even a third or fourth. The only thing keeping me in New York was the Marty Lyons Foundation. I also wanted to get into coaching. So I approached the Jets to see if I could work for them for free just to get in the door and get some coaching experience. My first attempt was a swing and miss. Strike one. I was told that I was too close to the team. Thank you but no thank you. After 12 years and seven operations, I was told that I couldn't work for free. That was hard to believe. My career with the Jets was over, so it was time to reflect on the appreciation I had for other individuals with whom I worked. I am forever indebted to the Hampton family for the love and friendship they showed me as a player.

The fans know the names and the numbers of the Jets players, but they don't know the guys in the locker room who makes going to work fun even after a loss on Sunday, and the Jets had one of the best equipment managers in all of sports in Bill Hampton, who was better known as Hamp. If you ask anyone who came through the Jets organization from the late 1960s to the end of the 1990s, the first face they saw coming into the complex was Hamp.

If you go home after having a bad day at the office, your dog is there waiting for you—happy as could be—to make your worst day seem great. Well, Hamp was kind of like that. He had seen it all and was with the team when they won Super Bowl III. Hamp covered for the players all the time. I remember walking into the complex a little hungover from the night before. So I took a quick shower and returned to my favorite napping place in the folding counter by the dryers. It was a great place for a quick power nap. You could hear the tumbling of the clothes in the dryer and feel the warmth of the heat, and Hamp was always there to wake you up so you didn't miss a meeting. Hamp's wife, Dottie, was a typical coach's wife. She'd seen it all, knew all the dirty little secrets about the players, and knew how to stop rumors before they got started. If you had a problem with your girlfriend or wife, you'd see Dottie. If they had a problem with you, you'd send them to Dottie, and she'd set them straight.

Hamp ran the equipment, but just like Batman, he had his Robin. Mickey Rendine was his sidekick. Rendine's favorite saying always ended with "young man." *How are you doing, young man? What's new, young man?* Rendine was a hard worker and a pleasure to be around. The love for Hamp and Rendine was so great that every Friday night we went to dinner together at an Italian restaurant named Mimmo's, which had great food. A few cocktails and a couple of rounds of poker made for a great Friday night. The respect we had for the both of them showed after an away game. As the equipment truck came back to the complex to be unloaded, a few of us would stay around and help Hamp unload the truck just so Hamp could finish his work faster and then go out with us. Beside Rendine and Hamp, we had Hamp's boys in the locker room all the time like Billy, Brian, Drew, Clay, and Derek.

Billy lived with me almost every year that I was with the Jets. He was a classic. Billy had a nickname for everyone. I was called Buffalohead, and Kyle Clifton was Jughead. Billy was great. I couldn't have asked for a better friend. Billy left the Jets, went to the Cleveland Browns, and then went to the NFL office. From the NFL office, he went to Under Armour. He had a great life. Billy was famous for making you feel important enough that he would take an order from you for shoes and sweat gear and then never send them. I still smile today about what a sales job he did on me every time. Billy died in 2011 of a massive heart attack. As the sad news went around like wildfire, all the memories came back to the surface. His sister, Beth, asked me if I would give his eulogy. It was such an honor to be chosen to celebrate Billy's life with a few words. I remember ending Billy's eulogy by saying, "Maybe we didn't say it loud enough and maybe we didn't say it often enough, but Billy, we love you." I also felt a great deal of love and respect for the entire Jets organization for all their support that they gave me for the Marty Lyons Foundation. They always said yes to supporting an event or bringing a child to practice.

I got a phone call from the hospital social worker to tell me that one of my kids, Joey, was in the hospital. Joey was the sweetest kid that you would ever want to meet. He lit up the room with his smile. He knew he was special and he knew he was sick. Joey would go in and out of the hospital to get treatment, and the hospital would call me when Joey refused to eat or take his medicine. I don't recall ever seeing Joey walk on his own. He always needed a pair of crutches, a walker, and later a wheelchair. Joey was only 4 years old when I met him, but he knew his platform in life. I used to tell Joey that if he gained five or six pounds, I would take him to see the Jets practice, and within a couple of days, the nurse would call and tell me that Joey was ready to see the team. Motivating a child with a trip to see the Jets was magical, and it made him feel special.

It was in the spring that I got the call that nobody ever wants to get. Joey was back in the hospital, but he was in a coma. I was there for three days with his parents when the doctors came in and said there was nothing more they could do. It was time to think about taking Joey off of life support. I knew that day would come one day, but I prayed to God that Joey would somehow recover and go into remission. I had an empty feeling when the parents turned to ask me what they should do. I didn't have the answer, but working with the kids from the foundation for almost 10 years taught me a lot about faith. I knew in my heart that God had a plan for Joey. As we gathered around the bed and Joey took his last breath, a smile came across his face, and then he was gone. I remember his father asking me, "Did you see that?"

I had. Joey was free of pain and running into heaven. I often think of Joey's strength and courage, never complaining and just living the life God gave him. Joey's parents were there from start to finish with their loving son. They were by his side all the time. As I continued to work with the children, I also realize the dedication the families had to make when their children were sick. They are the heroes we should be honoring. They were the role models we should try to be.

I worked a lot on the for the foundation in my first year of retirement in 1991. My golf game also got better, and I kept myself in shape in case the phone rang from a team that needed help due to an injury. I also had an opportunity to start a second career doing college football games as a broadcaster for Cablevision and the MSG Network. Doing the college game kept me in the game, and I stayed close to the Jets by working for them on Sundays in their hospitality suite. Watching the games from the suites was a lot different from being in the battlefield.

Coslet was still under the gun to win after going 6–10 the previous year. I didn't get to know Coslet that well since I was injured and then placed on injured reserve before the season. I wish I had. Coslet seemed like the type of coach for whom I would have enjoyed playing. I got to watch that draft class from 1989 grow as football players but more importantly as men of the community. When I got to the Jets in Jets in 1979, there was one old timer who spent a lot of time around the complex named John Schmitt. He was the center for the New York Jets when they won the Super Bowl back in 1969. Smitty was the picture perfect model of what you wanted to be after football. He was a successful businessman and well-respected in the community. That's what I wanted for myself and my family. I spent time talking with the players and giving them helpful tips so they could become better players and people.

The team had their highs and lows that season, finishing with a win against the Miami Dolphins the last game of the season to go 8–8 and get into the playoffs as a wild-card. The playoffs didn't last long as the Jets lost to the Houston Oilers, ending their season.

Lyons Life Lesson

Work hard at what you want in life, and sometimes people will make a decision for you that you don't like, that you can't fight. It just happens. Believe in yourself, realign your goals, and remember when one door closes, another door will open.

CHAPTER 12
Dennis Byrd and Boomer Esaison

During the 1992 season, I was still on the outside looking in. At this time I was only doing some appearances for the Jets and working in the hospitality suites on gameday. I was starting a second career off the field broadcasting college games, but I realized the phone wasn't going to ring from an NFL team, and my career as a football player was over. I was also getting a second chance at life when I married my wife, Christine.

Watching the Jets draft a tight end in the first round named Johnny Mitchel meant they were looking to upgrade that position to help Kenny O'Brien. What the Jets didn't realize was O'Brien was going to hold out at the start of the season for more money. O'Brien deserved every penny he could get. He had developed into a team leader, a quiet leader. He never complained about how many times he got sacked or how many times he got hit. He just did his job. I'd go into the trainer's room after a game, and he'd have six to eight bags of ice wrapped around different parts of his body.

When O'Brien got drafted in the first round back in 1983 right in front of Dan Marino, the fans were really disappointed because they wanted Marino. But it really didn't matter who they took until they fixed the offensive line. With O'Brien holding out for a new contract, it meant the Jets had to start their 1991 No. 1 pick, Browning Nagle out of Louisville. Nagle had a rifle of an arm and could really spin the ball. He was an all-around athlete. If you put a golf club in his hand, after 18 holes you were opening your wallet to pay your debt. With the heat on Bruce Coslet to follow up his 8–8 season, he knew it was time to win and time to produce. On paper the time looked good, but on the field it was totally different.

Throughout the previous season, I watched the games but had a special interest in one player, Dennis Byrd. He was growing into a Pro Bowl player. During his rookie season in 1989, he had seven sacks. In 1990 he had 13 sacks and in 1991 he had seven. He just continued to get better and better. But Byrd still had that one bad habit. He ducked his head upon impact.

The team went 4–12 in 1992, but the injuries the Jets experienced were life-changing. Al Toon received his ninth concussion in Week 10 and had to retire. And on November 29, Byrd broke his fifth cervical vertebrae. I remember watching the game on TV with Christine, and as soon as the play happened, it showed the replay, and I looked at Christine and said, "Dennis just broke his neck."

I went completely numb as tears rolled down my cheeks. The bad habit of ducking his head finally caught up with him.

Byrd was rushed to the hospital and had a procedure done where they drilled four holes into his skull and placed a halo ring around his head to immobilize his neck. I went to see him a day or two after the surgery. When I walked into his room, he was lying flat on his back with a pair of mirrored glasses on so he could see the person with whom he was talking without moving his head. The first thing Byrd said to me was: "I'm glad this happened to me rather than one of my teammates."

I asked why. He said he had faith that this was part of God's plan for him, that he was going to walk again, and that his teammates didn't have that kind of faith. Even as Byrd laid there in bed, he never lost faith. How could one individual be so strong and so committed? Byrd knew his days as a football player were over, but God was allowing him another platform, a bigger platform, and Byrd was getting ready to change the world one person at a time, starting with myself.

Byrd worked hard with extensive physical therapy, and a year later on September 5, 1993, he walked out on the field as an honorary New York Jets captain. I don't think that there was a dry eye in the entire stadium as the Jets fans gave Byrd a standing ovation, one he rightly deserved. In four years as a player, Byrd had 28 sacks and more than 100 tackles, but his new journey was just beginning.

He and I stayed in touch over the years. Whenever I called him to see how he was doing, he always had the ability to flip the conversation to how was I doing. Byrd cared about people. There was a term used in the 1970s and 1980s that a person of God was a "Bible Beater," always trying to convert as many people as possible. Byrd was the opposite with his faith. He knew that finding God was a process. He was there for you if you had a questions or needed guidance, but he never was forceful.

Byrd was an inspiration to the entire nation as he shared his story, but his story was more of an inspiration to the Jets family, and on October 28, 2012, the Jets made it official as they retired his No. 90. I remember walking out to the middle of the field with him that day. He came out of the tunnel in a golf cart and stopped at the 50-yard line where he met me. As we greeted and hugged each other, I walked him out to the microphone. At that point in Byrd's life, he was having trouble walking. So I put my arm around him and grabbed his belt for support. When we finally got out there, Byrd leaned over to me and said, "What should I say?" "Speak from the heart," I said. "That's what everyone wants you to do." When he finished we walked backed to the golf cart, told each other that we loved one another, and that we would stay in touch.

In 2010 Rex Ryan was the head coach of the Jets when they were making a playoff run and he brought Byrd in to talk to the team to inspire them the night before playing the New England Patriots in the AFC divisional round. The Jets had lost to New England 45–3 in Week 13. They needed something or someone to motivate them. They once again paid tribute to Byrd as the captains that day walked to midfield for the coin toss while holding Byrd's game jersey from 1992. I was doing the radio for the Jets that day and had a flashback to the play, in which he got hurt. The Jets defeated the Patriots 28–21, and seeing Byrd in the tunnel before and after the game was such a thrill.

As the Jets got ready to travel for a *Monday Night Football* game against the Arizona Cardinals in October of 2016, we left on Saturday to head west. When we arrived in Arizona, I got the news that Byrd had been killed in a car crash. My heart dropped. *How could this happen? Why did this happen? Was this part of God's plan?* I went back to my hotel room and choked back tears as I called his wife, Angela, not knowing what to say. I just found myself listening to the pain she was in. Every news channel relived Byrd's life from the time he got injured to the time he died. I truly believe that Byrd accomplished more in life after his injury than before it. He never lost faith, touched so many people, and had an impact on life.

As a member of the Jets family, I flew with owner Woody Johnson for the funeral. I delivered part of the eulogy. I reminded everyone of the impact Byrd had as a person. Byrd was always someone who wanted to be the best, and when Byrd got to the gates of heaven and was greeted by St. Peter, all he could say was, "How did I do? How did I do?" Those were the same lines he asked me back in 1989 after every practice. St Peter's answer was plain and simple, "Dennis, you couldn't have done a better job."

I miss Byrd and think of him often. He accomplished his mission in life and had an impact on all of us. There's a poem titled "The Dash" written by Linda Ellis, and she writes about the time in between when you were born and the day that you died or basically the dash between the year of birth and death on a tombstone. The final line of the poem reads, "So when your eulogy is being read, with your life's actions to rehash, would you be proud of the things they say about how you lived your dash?" Byrd should be very proud.

Byrd's life had such a tragic end, and I also endured sadness when my mother passed away in 1992. But I got to experience a life's beautiful beginning in 1993 when my son, Jesse, was born. Also during 1993 I was still on the outside looking in while working the Jets suites for home games and doing college games on the weekends for Cablevision. Coming off an injury-plagued 4–12 season in 1992, Coslet was going into his fourth year as the Jets head coach and was on the hot seat. He had to win. In the draft they added an outstanding middle linebacker in the first round out of Florida State named Marvin Jones, and he was very fortunate to sit and learn behind Kyle Clifton, who had been a roommate of mine early in his career after being drafted in the third round in 1984. Clifton wasn't just a physical player. He was a smart player. On the offensive side of the ball, Coslet was able to bring in a hometown hero, Boomer Esiason. The former Cincinnati Bengals quarterback grew up in New York. The Jets also brought in Johnny Johnson a former seventh-round pick in 1990 from the Phoenix Cardinals as their running back. It was a nice one-two punch and added leadership in the huddle and locker room. I had a chance to play against Esiason in my career and had a great deal of respect for him as a player and as a person. Even as a 32-year-old quarterback, he could still spin the ball. Esiason already had three Pro Bowl appearances and was NFL MVP in 1988, but how much did he have left in his tank and could he win with the Jets?

Once again tragedy hit a member of the Jets family. With the excitement of Esiason coming back to Long Island, it was also during his first minicamp with the Jets that he got the news that his 2-year-old son, Gunnar, was rushed to the hospital after having difficulty breathing. A few weeks later, Gunnar was diagnosed with cystic fibrosis. I was very familiar with it as I had worked with a group of kids at Stony Brook Hospital that all had that respiratory and digestive disease. I started off working with seven kids in a support group, and two years later, only one had survived. I couldn't imagine what Esiason was going through, or how he was going to be able to bounce back and play football.

Later that year Esiason started the Boomer Esiason Foundation with the mission of finding a cure for cystic fibrosis. Esiason not only put his name to the foundation, but he also put his money and more importantly his heart and soul into it. In 1995 the NFL honored him with the Walton Payton NFL Man of the Year award for those efforts. Thanks to Esiason, children are living longer, and a brighter tomorrow is on the horizon for families with children with cystic fibrosis.

In that 1993 season, the Jets added to the defensive side of the ball. A Pro Bowler, defensive lineman Leonard Marshall, came across town from the New York Giants, and a future Hall of Famer, Ronnie Lott, came aboard. Just the name of Ronnie Lott added excitement to the Jets. Watching Lott play was special. They don't make NFL players like Lott anymore. He was smart, physical, and a team leader.

Esiason ended the season with only 16 touchdown passes and had 11 interceptions, and once again the Jets missed the playoffs. Why couldn't the Jets turn things around? Was it time for another change at the head coaching position? Would owner Leon Hess make any other changes? There were a lot of questions but not a lot of answers. The Jets finished the season at 8–8. That record wasn't acceptable to the ownership or the fans. In the end Mr. Hess decided to let Coslet go after four years and an overall record of 26 38.

The final question was what would happen to Nagle, the quarterback of the future they drafted in 1991. Truth be told, Nagle never made the transition from a college quarterback to the needs of a NFL quarterback. You'll never hear me saying that a player was a bust, but when your team drafts players in the first or second round, those guys need to be impact playerd for years to come. Those players should become the foundation for the organization.

Lyons Life Lesson

If you want someone to like and respect you, you must like and respect yourself first. Feel good about who you are.

CHAPTER 13
The Pete Carroll and Rich Kotite Eras

Getting ready for the 1994 season was interesting as the Jets promoted their defensive coordinator Pete Carroll to head coach. With Carroll now at the helm, I took my second swing at becoming a coach for the New York Jets. Carroll was my last defensive coordinator I played for in 1990 with the Jets. Unfortunately, that was the season I tore my bicep and missed the entire season. I believed that Carroll knew I wanted to get into coaching and I was limited where I could go to get the coaching experience I needed because my foundation was based in New York.

I went to the Jets complex on a Friday unannounced to talk with Carroll, who was running around. We briefly spoke, and the conversation ended with Carroll telling me to come back on Monday. "I think I can help you," he said. Those words made my weekend as I looked forward to our meeting on Monday.

On Monday I got to Carroll's office early and waited for him to come in for our meeting. I waited and waited, and when Carroll finally came in, he apologized. He said he had completely forgotten and was in the gym playing basketball. That was no big deal to me. But to my surprise when I asked him about working for the Jets and coaching for free, he said, "You really don't want to coach. If you want to help the Jets, go down to the PR department and tell me how we can get our players more active in the community."

I was stunned. *What just happened?* Maybe Carroll was smarter than I, maybe that's where I could've helped the team the most, but it wasn't what I wanted. I wanted to coach. I was at the plate taking a swing at coaching, and strike two arrived before I could even take the bat off my shoulder.

To his credit, Carroll was an individual who had the pedal to the metal all the time. He interacted with the players, was a great motivator, and loved the game of football. Carroll put together an outstanding staff and also had Pat Kirwan as the assistant director of pro personnel. But he had an aging quarterback in Boomer Esiason who needed to stand upright in the pocket to complete his throws. Going 4–5 in their first nine games wasn't bad nor was it good. That was also the year that Miami Dolphins quarterback Dan Marino used the fake spike against the Jets defense. It was an outstanding play by Marino and a complete breakdown by the defense. After that game the team just went completely south, losing six of its last seven games, ending the season with a 6–10 record. Carroll was fired after one season. He was the fall guy for the lack of accountability of the players. One year to build your own program and you get fired? That doesn't seem fair.

That call was ultimately made by the owner, but I loved Leon Hess. He was nothing but good to me and my family. Mr. Hess wanted to win so badly for the organization and the fans. I remember all the little things he did to show team unity like our Thanksgiving dinners at the Diamond Club at Shea Stadium. He wanted the families of the players to meet one another. He always came out to my swarm party at the end of training camp to support the team. When I started my foundation in 1982, Mr. Hess was right there again showing his support of the team to my mission. He was special, and I'm sure that the players who worked for him would agree that we're sorry we didn't win a Super Bowl for him before he sold the team. Mr. Hess was loyal to his players and just wanted to win.

The firing of Carroll meant that the Jets would have three different head coaches in as many years, which is obviously not good. To build a winning attitude and culture, you must have stability at the top.

The Jets announced Rich Kotite as their next head coach in 1995. Kotite was the wide receiver coach when I played and then became the head coach of the Philadelphia Eagles. He was always one of Mr. Hess' favorite people. I was the only former player at the press conference that day to show support for him. Kotite and I had been good friends since my playing days and we even played in each other's charity golf tournaments.

I still had that burning desire in me to coach, so maybe Kotite was the guy to hire me.

I met with Kotite the next week about the possibility of joining his staff. He said he could not hire me because I lacked coaching experience. It seemed like total bullshit to me. That was strike three, game over, time to move on. My coaching dreams were over.

On the bright side, my family was growing and so was my foundation. My daughter, Megan, was born in November of 1994, and the foundation operated in roughly six states with no paid employees, and wishes were at an all-time high. It was at this time that I had so many families coming to the foundation looking for a second wish, meaning their child had a relapse, and they needed help once again. I kept telling them that I wanted to help, but their child already had a wish. After telling parents that answer for years, I went to my board of directors and asked them to think about changing our bylaws and allowing us to do a second wish when further medical issues occurred. With money in our

My daughter, Megan, was born in 1994. She hangs out with her brothers Lucas (left) and Jesse (right) during the holidays.

endowment account, we decided to be different. The only issue was raising more money to keep up with the funding process for the children's wishes.

In the years to come, we would see more second wishes then first wishes. We even got labeled as a second-wish foundation by many. It didn't matter to me what we were called. I just knew in my heart that I couldn't keep denying families only because they had used a previous wish. Put yourself in the shoes of these families. When you find out your child is sick, your world is crushed. And then when they go into remission, you feel the hope and prayers have paid off. When your child then has a relapse, words can't describe the feelings they experience.

I got a call from Bobby Parente of the Jets asking me if I would be interested in hosting the in-house TV show, *Jets Journal*. I thought it would be a great opportunity for me to grow as a broadcaster. Plus it would give me insight to the thinking of the organization from the players to the coaches. But I didn't want anything to happen to Dave Jennings, the host who played for both the New York Giants and the Jets. I had I great deal of respect for him. My first phone call was to him, letting him know about the possibility of doing the show and to tell him I didn't want to go behind his back. Jennings appreciated the call, wished me luck, and thanked me.

What a blast it was doing that show with my cohost Al Trautwig, who had worked for every major network, including hosting the Ironman Championship and the Olympics. To be successful as a broadcaster, you must have chemistry with your partner, and Trautwig was the best. He took me under his wing and made the show more about having fun while still being informative about the Jets. My responsibilities included interviewing the head coach on what happened in last week's game, discussing what to look forward to in the upcoming game, and doing a few stand-up segments with Trautwig on different topics.

The start of my broadcast career with the Jets came in 1995, and the first coach I got to work with was the same guy who wouldn't give me a chance to coach, my friend, Kotite. He had been the head coach for the Eagles for four years, posted an overall record of 37–29, took the Eagles to the playoff twice, and had two seasons where his team won double digits game in the tough NFC East. Bringing Kotite back to the Jets was a homecoming for him. He was from Staten Island and coached the Jets wide receivers in 1983 and 1984 before being promoted to the offensive coordinator, a role he served from 1985 to 1989. He knew the lay of the land in New York and he also knew the media here. So it seemed like it might be a perfect fit.

With every new head coach the Jets brought in, new expectations and goals were set, but one goal never changed: get to the playoffs. The season outlook looked good. With the first pick, they drafted Kyle Brady, a tight end out of Penn State. On paper this was a great move. Brady was 6'6" and weighed 270 pounds. He could catch and block, and the Jets hadn't had that in a productive tight end since Mickey Shuler, who also played at Penn State. In the first round, they also drafted a defensive end named Hugh Douglas who was a stud.

The best acquisition was when the Jets gave a free-agent contract to Wayne Chrebet. I was so happy for him. He was a good kid with a big heart and could play football with the best of them. Only 5'10" Chrebet was a standout for Hofstra University. I got to cover him for four years because I was doing the games for MSG and Cablevision. I'll never forget his last game against Delaware. He had five touchdowns and about 250 yards. After that game I told his parents to get their son an agent because he could play in the NFL. Chrebet started off as the 11th receiver in Jets training camp that year, but he worked hard every day. With injuries to others, he worked his way up the depth chart. Chrebet was a local kid, who had fans coming out to watch practice daily. They were rooting for the underdog to make the team, and he did that by the end of training camp.

My routine was very simple for *Jets Journal*, but if the Jets were losing, those interviews with the coach got harder and harder. After the first couple of losses, the interviews weren't just about the coach, it was also about me creating credibility with the fans. I learned early not to use the term "we." My days of playing were over, and it was about the current players and the current condition of the team. There were interviews I did that year with Kotite, where I would give him a softball question rather than a hardball question out of respect for him and the organization. After all, the season was a complete disaster. It ended with a 3–13 record, which set a franchise record for the most losses in one season.

One of the biggest things that I saw in this team was the lack of discipline, and it started at practice. Watching the players while they stretched told the entire story. Players did what they wanted to do and didn't seem like they were on the same page. Was this lack of discipline coming from the way Kotite ran his camp, or was it the lack of discipline from the players themselves? My guess is that it was a little of both. Where was the accountability on both sides? The buck starts and stops with the head coach, but some of the blame must go back onto the players. This is the NFL, and you get paid to win games. If Kotite was going to be around for the 1996 season, he had to make some adjustments to turn his team into a contender.

Loyalty won out, and Mr. Hess decided to give Rich and his staff another season. Not sure if that was the way to go, but I liked Kotite as a person, and I wanted to see the team win, turn this thing around, and have some stability at the top. The team also needed to put a better product on the field for their fans. During that 3–13 season, fans were leaving at halftime because the team was terrible.

Around the same time, I was inducted into the Suffolk Sports Hall of Fame on Long Island. In that class there was nine inductees, and at the dinner we were told to keep our speeches to three to five minutes. With a packed house, they walked us in, and I was scheduled to be the last inductee of the evening. When I got up to accept my honor, half the tables were empty, so I started off with the joke that I knew the committee put me last because I played for the Jets, and we were always used to the crowd leaving before the game was over. It was sad but true. Call it the ripple effect. What happens on the practice field carries over to the games and offseason events.

What people don't realize is pro athletes are just like them. We put on our pants the same way, and the pain we feel when we lose a loved one is the same as yours. I got a phone call from my sister, Theresa, in 1995 that my oldest brother and his wife, Sharon, lost their 16-year-old son, Christopher. He was loved by all. He was a good kid with a bright future. As all parents do, they blamed themselves. My brother was no different. He asked himself what he could have done to prevent the accident. The simple answer is nothing. My hope is that Christopher knew in his heart how much he was loved, and that one day that void in my brother's heart will be filled. When we lose a parent it's hard, but the loss of a child is unbearable.

The Lyons family is close, and we suffered a great loss in 1995.

* * *

After going 3–13 the year before, the Jets received the No. 1 over-all pick in the 1996 NFL Draft and selected wide receiver Keyshawn Johnson out of USC. Johnson was a talent ready for the NFL. He had four things that you always look for in a receiver: great character, great hands, speed, and a love and commitment to the game of football. You almost feel sorry for those outstanding college players who go to the worst NFL team, believing that they are the answer to all the previous problems. They aren't. They're one of 53 players who must play as a team and build chemistry to win in the NFL.

Boomer Esiason was gone in 1996 and he spent more time on his back then he did in an upright position anyway. Sometimes it's not how many times you get sacked. It's how many times you get hit. You know you're in trouble when after the ball was snapped that your offensive line-man yell, "watch out." It means someone missed a blocked.

New at the quarterback position was Neil O'Donnell, who showed he could take a team on his shoulders and take them to the Super Bowl as he did with the Pittsburgh Steelers. His backup was a previous seventh-round pick, Glenn Foley.

I've always believed you must start fast in the NFL to make it to the playoffs, and the Jets did everything but that, starting a woeful 0–8. It meant that the pressure at the Jets complex in Hempstead, New York, was building. Everyone was looking over their shoulders to see if they were the next one out the door. Doing *Jets Journal* wasn't easy either. The interviews with Rich Kotite became harder and harder and so did the questions.

One day we were interviewing Kotite in his office. It was a two-camera shoot. One was on him, and the other was on me as I asked the questions. Our director was Andrew Braun, and being a perfectionist, he always wanted to capture the best pictures. We did the same routine every Wednesday and reviewed the questions beforehand to make sure we weren't crossing over the line. At 0–3 or maybe even 0–4, you could still get away with the easy questions and ask homer questions like, "Richie, I know your team played hard. What can you do to turn this thing around?" But at 0–8 we also needed to show the fans that we were holding ourselves accountable.

Braun noticed a problem with our setup. The tree he had in his office made it look like it was growing out of Kotite's head, so we moved it a couple of feet back. As the interview started, we recapped their ninth straight loss. I don't remember any of the other questions I asked that day, but I hit a nerve with Kotite. When the interview was over and the cameras stopped shooting, Kotite went off, and, I mean, he went off. He was yelling at me about who the fuck did I think I was, asking those type of questions to him on his TV show. First, I reminded him it wasn't his show. It was the Jets' show, and, secondly, I reminded him that his team was 0–8. What did he expect me to ask him? As he was leaving his office, he turned as red as an apple and yelled one last thing, "Who the fuck moved my tree?" Yes, tensions were at an all-time high.

The Jets finished the season 1–15, a new franchise worst. Kotite resigned as the head coach. The loyalty of Mr. Hess again showed up. Just as they told me after the 1990 season, when the Jets said I could retire with class or be cut tomorrow, Kotite had the choice of resigning or being fired. Kotites's overall record in two seasons with the Jets was 4–28. I truly believed that the one item that Kotite took for granted was discipline. Kotite isn't a bad guy. He does a lot in the Staten Island community. Maybe his coaching methods would have worked on a more veteran team, but the bottom line was he just wasn't able to win football games. They say there are two types of coaches in the NFL: those who have been fired, and those who will be fired. Maybe we should add a third category for those whose resign. So much for coaching experience.

The 1996 season was bleak, but it had a great moment for me. I was blessed with a fourth child when my son, Luke, was born in October. All my kids were good at whatever they put their minds to. Rocky played baseball, Jesse played soccer, Megan was into gymnastics, and Luke played soccer. But what was more impressive was they all excelled in school, something with which I struggled. Thank God for mom.

People always have asked me if I was disappointed my boys didn't play football. How could I be disappointed when Rocky became a doctor, Jesse became a doctor, Megan became a schoolteacher, and Luke became an aerospace engineer? You couldn't ask for better results from your kids than I have received. I'm truly blessed.

Lyons Life Lesson

Show respect for others and show respect for yourself. Encourage your children to be the best that they can be, facilitate their needs, guide them along their journey. Remember it's their life not yours. It's their dreams not yours and show them love and support in good times and bad. Accept them for who they are.

CHAPTER 14
The Bill Parcells Era

After the past two seasons, Jets fans demanded a better product on the field in 1997. The Jets knew that they needed someone who had a proven track record and someone who could evaluate talent, but more than anything, they needed someone who demanded respect and would instill discipline both on and off the field. In everyone's mind there was only one choice: Bill Parcells. But the question was how to pry him away from the New England Patriots.

The Jets hired Parcells as a special advisor to the new head coach, Bill Belichick. *Wink, Wink.* New England didn't want any of that, so it complained to the NFL league office and the commissioner, who brokered a deal that allowed Parcells to be the head coach with the Jets and gave New England a future draft pick for the coach. As a result of this transaction, Belichick was the official head coach of the Jets for six days, and the Jets had their man in Parcells.

I didn't know much about Parcells except that he demanded a lot, and he got results. As an NFL player, that's what you want from your head coach. You want to work hard so that you have a chance to make it to the playoffs and win the Super Bowl. Parcells checked all those boxes when he was with the New York Giants, and they won Super Bowl XXI and Super Bowl XXV.

In 1988 we scrimmaged the Giants before the first preseason game. That scrimmage was normally filled with a lot of fights, individual pass rush drills, and 7-on-7 drills. The Giants in 1988 drafted a mountain of a man in the second round named Jumbo Elliott. He was 6'7" and weighed more than 300 pounds. It was during the pass rush drills that I got to see how Parcells motivated his players and got the most out of them. I was going up against Elliott one on one when I knocked his hands down during the drill and got to the quarterback. Parcells barked out at Elliott, "Jumbo, this isn't college any more. Lyons is going to wear you a new ass. Do it again."

So at his request, we reset at the line of scrimmage. The ball was snapped, and this time, I made an inside move to get around Elliott, and it worked. Parcells was now riding Elliott, barking out, "Do it again." The third time I wasn't so lucky. I did an out move and then an inside move. It was time to bull rush him and try to run him over. I went straight for Elliott. I extended my hands toward his chest when he ducked his head. I got my right index finger stuck in his facemask and twisted his head. As Elliott twisted, so did my finger. I dislocated it at the middle joint. As I was yelling in pain, all I could hear was Parcells barking at Elliott, "Good job, Jumbo! That's what you must do every play."

The discipline with the team started with the stretching period. There were straight lines with everyone in a row, and all the players had their helmets on the right side. Start with the little things, and the big things will fall into place.

I was still doing *Jets Journal*, and in my first interview with Parcells, he set the ground rules in a very subdued way. He made sure no equipment was running when he looked at me and said quietly, "Marty, everyone in this room has skeletons in their closet, but you my friend, you own a graveyard."

I was kind of taken back by his comment and politely asked, "Why's that?"

Parcells answered my question with a old story involving a flight attendant, and I said okay. Coach and I were on the same page. The respect that I had for this man all these years just got bigger. Parcells didn't do it to embarrass me, but it was all part of his ability to get inside one's head. I enjoyed and looked forward to our one-on-one meeting every Wednesday. Parcells was open about the team and he trusted me with inside information, knowing that I knew what I could use and what I couldn't. Parcells always took it a step or two more at the end of the interview, telling me he needed me for short-yardage defense. I actually believed him, often thinking to myself, *Maybe I could play six-to-seven*

My radio crew poses with Hall of Famer Richard Dent (in the navy sweater and jeans). I interviewed another Hall of Famer, Bill Parcells, every Wednesday during his tenure coaching the Jets.

plays a game. But then I would be brought back to reality when producer Bobby Parente would tell me, "You do know he's messing with you."

If Parcells had the ability to motivate an old, washed-up player like myself, what could he do with young talented players? The answer was a lot.

That year the Jets turned around the season and the organization's mind-set, going 9–7. They could have been better because they lost the last two games of the season, but everyone felt good about the direction the team was heading—even the long suffering Jets fans.

Coming off a 9–7 season after going 4–28 under Richie Kotite, the Jets were feeling pretty good about the direction the team was moving in, heading into the 1998 season. Parcells had made a comment in New England that ruffled a few feathers but seemed appropriate for the Jets front office. He said, "If they want you to cook the dinner, at least they ought to let you shop for some of the groceries."

It was a classic line. Parcells knew the type of players he wanted, but he also knew the type of players he could coach. That's what made him so special. One thing the players knew and understood: playing for Parcells wasn't always easy, but if you did what he asked you to do, you gave yourself a chance to win in the fourth quarter. Discipline wasn't a problem any more. There was only one man in charge, and that was Parcells.

The groceries were about to be delivered starting with a new quarterback, Vinny Testaverde. He was nothing but class with a capital C, and who could forget that Testaverde won the Heisman Trophy in 1986 as the best colligate player in the nation? Testaverde had a great year and went on to throw for 29 touchdowns and only seven interceptions. Parcells went out and worked a deal to get future Hall of Famer running back Curtis Martin. Like Testaverde, Martin was a man with class and character. Parcells also knew the game was won in the trenches. So he then went out and got future Hall of Famer Kevin Mawae, who was a unique player. The nicest guy off the field, he was nasty when he got on the field but in a clean way. Whatever he talked on the field, he could back it up. It never surprised me to see No. 68 down the field getting a block long after the play crossed the line of scrimmage.

The Jets also had a one-two punch at the wide receiver position with Wayne Chrebet and Keyshawn Johnson. Chrebet had developed into the go-to guy in the slot on third down, and getting popped over the middle was just part of going to work for him. Defensively, the Jets had guys up front who could get to the quarterback, but you also had linebackers like Mo Lewis and Pepper Johnson who came to play every down. Don't forget the Jets had Bill Belichick running the defense. That can never be undervalued.

The 1998 Jets went 12–4 and won the AFC East for the first time since the AFL-NFL merger in 1970. Two years removed from 1–15, the Jets had a bye week to get ready for the divisional playoff game, and their opponent turned out to be the Jacksonville Jaguars.

Parcells had his team ready both physically and mentally. The Jets jumped out to a 17-point lead before Jacksonville could get on the scoreboard. New York went into half with a 17–7 lead. And even with three turnovers that day, the Jets came away with a 34–24 victory.

The Jets were one game away from the Super Bowl, but anything can happen at that point. I was a part of an AFC Championship Game against the Miami Dolphins when the field was muddy and wet. I knew the excitement of that week. Everyone starts making Super Bowl plans and thinking about tickets, hotels, etc., while you still had to focus on the AFC Championship Game. The Jets had to travel to Denver to play the Broncos and John Elway, one of the best quarterbacks to ever play the game and a future Hall of Famer.

The air was cold and light as we landed in Denver. Some players always found it hard to breathe because of the altitude. I found it to be just another excuse you could use if your team lost. The Jets didn't play well in the first half but still managed to take a 3–0 lead into the locker room at halftime. I was sitting in the stands, freezing my ass off but feeling pretty good about their chances in the second half if they cleaned up the little things. That was also something that Parcells was good at: pointing something out and cleaning it up. The third quarter started with a Jets touchdown to put New York up 10–0. The Broncos fans were sitting on their hands. Not only was it cold, but their team wasn't playing well. Then it happened. Elway threw a touchdown pass to make it 10–7. Then Denver kicked a field goal to make it 10–10.

The sleeping giants had come back alive. Denver went on to score 23 unanswered points to win 23–10. Testaverde outplayed Elway that day, throwing for more 350 yards while Elway threw for a little more than 170 yards and one touchdown. The biggest problem was the Jets had six costly turnovers! The Jets would have to wait another year before they could possibly make another run at the title. But there are no guarantees in the NFL. Every year brings different faces to the team, and faces would be missing from the previous team because they moved on or they were cut.

Even though they lost in the AFC Championship Game, the buzz in the offseason was back because of the way the Jets finished up. If the Jets had Parcells, things were going to be just fine.

With all the excitement of the 1998 season, the players, coaches, organization, and the fans couldn't wait for the 1999 season. They had been one game away from going to the Super Bowl, and Elway, the quarterback of the team who had defeated them, had retired. The *Jets Journal* show was going well, and each week I felt that the trust between myself and Coach Parcells was getting stronger. But then tragedy would ensue.

On February 15 Vinny Testaverde's father, Al, passed away. I knew how close Vinny was to his father because I had that same relationship with my own. They were best friends.

Then in May of 1999, the entire NFL and Jets organization lost a friend when Jets owner Leon Hess passed away at the age of 85. I always had a great relationship with Mr. Hess as a player and then after I retired. He was an honest man with a big heart. He loved the people of New York and he loved his team. Make no mistake, Mr. Hess was a true businessman running the Hess Corporation, so I'm sure that the men sitting on the opposite side of the table may have a different opinion of him.

When Mr. Hess died, the ownership of the team went into the Hess Estate, meaning it was going to be sold with the approval of the owners and the NFL. I always thought that his son, John, would take over the team if something happened to Mr. Hess, but he wanted John to have complete control of the Hess Corporation not the world of football.

The 1999 draft brought another piece to the offensive line when they drafted Randy Thomas in the second round out of Mississippi State. This was perfect for the Jets; he was able to learn from the best center, Mawae.

Training camp opened that year with the crowd being at an all-time high. The players came back in shape ready to go, preparing for their season opener against the Patriots.

The only thing that could hold this team back was injuries. They didn't have the proper depth at some positions, and Parcells was working on that. The one player the Jets had to keep healthy was Testaverde. Then on Opening Day on a freak play, Testaverde ruptured his Achilles and was lost for the season. Later in the game, running back Leon Johnson tore two ligaments in his knee, ending his season. Now Parcells had to move forward with a backup plan at the quarterback position, which wouldn't be easy.

My weekly interviews with Parcells were going well. He was open, engaging, and had a great sense of humor, considering the endless and frustrating problem of finding a replacement for Testaverde.

The rotation of punter/quarterback Tom Tupa and Rick Mirer didn't work after the first 10 games. With a record of 4–6, Parcells turned the quarterback position over to the third-string quarterback, Ray Lucas, who was an undrafted quarterback out of Rutgers. He had spent time with Parcells in New England, and Parcells loved Lucas. He was tougher than Brillo, and the Jets could use him at any position on the field. He might not have been the best player out there, but you could count on him giving 100 percent. Before the Wildcat formations became popular, Parcells put Lucas in at quarterback in 1997 and took O'Donnell and moved him to a wide receiver in 1997. Lucas took the direct snap and ran for 15 yards and a first down. Lucas lost his first game as a starter but then won four in a row, and the Jets finished at 8–8.

It was late in October on a Wednesday when I went over to the complex to interview Parcells for a weekly spot, and I noticed that Parcells wasn't himself. Something was on his mind. After we did the show, we sat around and talked about the terrible plane crash that happened on Monday that took the life of PGA golfer Payne Stewart and the other four passengers on the plane. One of those passengers was a young man named Robert Fraley. He was a backup quarterback at Alabama when I was a freshman. I didn't know him well, but I remember he went on to become an agent. Fraley came to me after my senior year and wanted to represent me prior to the NFL draft. He told me he would do it for $500. I don't know why I turned down his offer, but I did. I also turned down an offer to be represented by Jimmy Walsh, who represented both Joe Namath and Richard Todd. To this day I regret not choosing one of them. What I didn't know at the time was Fraley represented Parcells. After hearing that from Parcells, I could understand the pain he had in his heart. He didn't just lose his agent; he lost a friend. I had never seen that side of Parcells. The tough guy, that hard ass coach, sat there with tears in his eyes and his voice cracking while talking about his friend.

With the season coming to an end, rumors started to surface that Parcells was going to step down after three seasons with the Jets and be an advisor for the team and the next owner and promote defensive coordinator Belichick to be the next head coach of the Jets. And at the end of the season, that's exactly what happened—except it didn't last too long. Patriots owner Bob Kraft made Belichick an offer he couldn't refuse. For the second time in four years, Belichick was the head coach of the Jets and never coached a single game! Next in line was Al Groh, the linebacker's coach, and he accepted the position to be the head coach of the Jets for the 2000 season.

I hated to see Parcells leave the field. He brought back respect to the organization and what he did with the talent despite the injuries was unbelievable.

Meanwhile, the Marty Lyons Foundation was growing. I was still able to do all the work with volunteers and was getting ready to change my own career path. I left PaineWebber after five years and started work for an athletic field construction company named Landtek, which was privately owned by Mike Ryan and Greg Sharpe. I had a handshake agreement that I would help them grow their company and they would help me grow the foundation. When people started to bitch about not having a project done on time, I would always go visit a child or a family from the foundation to keep in touch with what was important in life.

I got a wish application from a family in Glenn Cove, Long Island, requesting a generator for their house. I also noticed that this family had two children who were sick. So on a rainy day with every client complaining about their fields getting done, I made a trip to the north shore to meet the family.

As I knocked on the door, the mother answered the door carrying a beautiful little boy that had to be around 2 years old. I told her who I was, and she asked me if I wanted to meet her boys. As we walked up the stairs, I never expected to see what was behind the bedroom doors when she opened them. Laying in two single beds were her twins. Both were on life support machines while a 24-hour nurse sat there writing up reports. She introduced me to her twin boys. As we were talking, one of the boys started to have a seizure, and the nurse reacted quickly to calm him down. She went back to her notes and reported what had just happened. The mom and I went back downstairs to talk, and I asked her why she requested a generator. "As you can see, my boys are both on life support, and we lose power quite a bit," she said. "A couple of weeks ago, we lost power for some time."

If the power didn't come on, she would have to decide which of the boys should she resuscitate first. I went back to the car and was completely numb. I had to do something. I started making phone calls, and the kindness in people's heart came pouring out. Within an eight-week period, all the donors were there to cut the ribbon as the house now had a backup generator to power her house.

Lyons Life Lesson

Have you ever found yourself in a situation where you lost contact with a good friend and wonder why it happened? Well, it happens to all of us. It's nobody's fault. It's life. There is no doubt it hurts when you lose a friendship. Maybe it was something you said or something you did, but more than likely it wasn't a true friendship to begin with. A friendship is like a conversation. It's shared in both directions. One person can't put more into the relationship than the other and get less of a return.

Remember to be yourself, love yourself, and respect yourself. Treat people the way you want to be treated. It doesn't matter the color of a person skin, the sexuality of a person, the religious beliefs of a person, or the political party of a person. You have to accept people for who they are. I've traveled around the world and talked to a lot of high school students about bullying others. It's a real problem that affect hundreds of thousands of kids a year, and it must stop. If it doesn't stop, where are our future generations of kindness going to come from? We must continue to educate our youth and be an example for them to learn from.

CHAPTER 15
Franchise Turnover

The 2000 season was the first year under new ownership after Woody Johnson bought the team. A fan of the game, Johnson was like a kid in the candy store. He was competitive and wanted the best for his team and the fans. If Johnson was going to win, he had to leave the grocery shopping to one person, Bill Parcells, the same person who brought the Jets back to NFL respectability. And that's what he did.

Parcells went right to work in the front office. He knew he needed more talent in the locker room to win, but he also knew he needed impact players who could play right away. He started with the draft, trading players away like Keyshawn Johnson for draft choices. When all was said and done, Parcells had four first-round picks in the 2000 draft. The Jets took two defensive players in Shaun Ellis from Tennessee and John Abraham from South Carolina, who were both edge rushers. And on the offensive side of the ball, they took Chad Pennington, a quarterback out of Marshall, and got Anthony Becht, a tight end out of West Virginia. That might have been the best draft class in the history of the franchise. If you include wide receiver Laveranues Coles in the third round, it truly was a draft class that was special.

Al Groh was not Parcells, and he knew it. Groh didn't try to be anyone but himself. Groh was 100 percent business, and I respected that. Like Parcells, all he wanted to do was win.

With three games to go in the 2000 season, the Jets looked like they were a shoe-in for the playoffs with a 9–4 record. Then they lost their last three games to finish the season at 9–7. Sure, it was better than the year before, but it wasn't good enough for anyone in the organization. Everyone wondered why the Jets couldn't win in December.

To make matters worse, Groh got an offer to become the next head coach at his alma mater, the University of Virginia. I was happy for Groh. He was a great guy who had hired his son to be on his staff. It gave him job security for his family. Groh was a football coach to the core and would do great things for those young college-athletes.

Shortly after Groh left, Parcells stepped down from the operatiosn side of the Jets front office and retired from football.

The talent was in place for the Jets, but they needed to find a new leader.

While the Jets looked for a new head coach and general manager, my career as a broadcaster was moving forward. I got hired by the Jets to be the color analyst for their radio broadcast. I had the pleasure of working with one of the best up-and-coming broadcasters in the field, Bob Wischusen. I remember talking to Al Trautwig, my partner from *Jets Journal*, about the difference between doing radio and TV. He had great advice. "When you're doing radio, pretend you're talking to a blind person. Paint the picture," he said. "Your listening audience can't see the game. So you must create the picture through your words. Trust your partner."

He stressed that last point, and over the last 18 years, I couldn't have asked for a better one than Wischusen. He is professional and talented, and the friendship we have built over the years reflects the respect we have for one another.

Traveling with the team was special. Interviewing the players and coaches leading up to the game was challenging but beneficial because we were basically an extension of the team. I enjoyed meeting the players on a more personal level and being that extension from the team to the fan. Back in the studio, we had Greg Buttle as an analyst and Don LaGreca as a great professional. Bobby Parente from the Jets office put together a combination of talent that really worked. The games were fun because the guys you worked with respected each other. Everyone had a role.

Working for the team that drafted me, I often ask myself, *Do you believe in fate?* My wife, Christine, is a firm believer that things happen for a reason. Why did I get drafted by the New York Jets in 1979 and not one of the other 31 NFL teams? Why did God place me in the media capital of the world rather than a place like Cleveland? Why did God allow my father to die four days after my oldest son, Rocky, was born and then two days later take a 5-year old boy out of my life? Those six days opened my life to helping children with a terminal illness. That was my calling. My fate was using the platform of playing in the NFL in New York to make that happen.

Another fateful encounter occurred when I was leaving a meeting and walking back to my car, which was parked around the corner. I cut through the courtyard for some reason, even though I wasn't in a hurry. About halfway in the courtyard, I saw a lady sitting on a bench with her sunglasses on. When I got within speaking distance, I told her it was a great day to catch some rays. She agreed and then asked if I was Marty Lyons and went on to tell me that the foundation sent her and her daughter to Walt Disney World and that she never had a chance thank me. Her daughter passed away right after their trip. I told her how sorry I was, but she said the foundation provided great memories.

* * *

The Jets decided to put their fate in Herm Edwards, a football guy with great character. Edwards was one of the nicest gentlemen I've ever met on and off the field. He had a strong personality, faith, leadership abilities and knew how to motivate people. Edwards became famous for a one-line response to a question in a press conference, "You play to win the game." That wasn't just his approach to the game of football. It was his approach to the game of life.

Edwards inherited a pretty good team, a team that was built by Parcells and was ready to make another run at the playoffs. The Jets finished 10–6 that season, one game better than the 9–7 record the year before, but both the New England Patriots and the Miami Dolphins finished 11–5, one win ahead of the Jets. The good news was they made

A football guy with great character, Herm Edwards is one of the nicest gentle-men I've ever met. (New York Jets)

the playoffs. The bad news was they had to go to "The Black Hole" in Oakland to play the Raiders in the wild-card game.

The Jets lost to the Raiders 38–24, but it seemed like they were moving in the right direction. The 2001 draft brought in quality players such as Santana Moss, LaMont Jordan, and Kareem McKenzie. And they had a head coach in Edwards who could motivate, though in a different way than Parcells did. Edwards was more of a soft-spoken coach who was always on point with his words. The players loved him, and it seemed like they respected him. But this was the Jets, and anything could happen.

I had a great relationship with Edwards, and as part of the radio team, we met with him once a week to go over the upcoming game and player information such as who was playing and who wasn't. Edwards treated us with respect. He knew that the radio team was just an extension of the club, and we knew what information we could use and what information wasn't for public knowledge. We would spend about an hour with Edwards, asking questions, and Edwards always started his reply with "Now, Coach." It was an endearing sign of respect. Edwards believed in giving back to the community and played in a lot of charity events, including mine.

I really got to know and respect Edwards as person when I got him involved in a wish for a 17-year-old boy named Steven. He came down with a brain tumor in between his junior and senior year of high school and was so sick that he couldn't take the trip the foundation had planned for him. Steven had lost close to 50 pounds from his chemotherapy treatments and had a large trash can next to his bed because he had to throw up so frequently. Steven knew his role in life, accepted it, and now he was sharing it with me. On the second visit with Steven, I took Edwards. The head coach brought a Jets bag filled with goodies, and as we drove from the Jets headquarters to Steven's house, we talked about life, not football. When we got to the house, I introduced Edwards. Coach was unbelievable. He talked about football, life, and faith. After about 30 minutes, we were getting ready to leave, and Edwards told Steven if he needed anything to reach out. "Could you call my dad?" Steven then asked. "He's a really big Jets fan."

Edwards then walked over to the house phone and called his father at work and talked for a good 10 minutes. We said our good-byes, and Edwards and I got back in the car. I remarked that when Steven asked if he could call his father, he reminded us to think of others before we thought of ourselves.

The entire world was impacted on September 11, 2001, when our nation was attacked by terrorists, killing almost 3,000 innocent individuals, shattering dreams of families, and leaving broken hearts that would never be repaired.

It's crazy to think the day before the attack on September 10, I was in the South Tower at 7:30 AM working a United Way fair, recruiting individuals to donate through payroll deduction to their favorite charity.

I was sitting in my office at Landtek the next morning when the first plane crashed into the north tower. When the second plane crashed into the south tower, I left the office and went and picked my kids up from school. Glued to the TV, I couldn't believe the horror as the day played out.

Thank God for the individuals on Flight 93 that left Newark, New Jersey, heading toward Washington, D.C. They forced that plane to crash into a field in Pennsylvania, or the death toll would have been higher. Those brave men and women, who fought the hijackers, saved lives while sacrificing their own. I went to Ground Zero twice, and each time I left with so much anger. When you're at war, lives will be lost. When you go to work or you send you children to school, you expect them to come home safe, and when they don't, something is wrong. As days passed, the search for survivors continued, and as days went to months, bodies were being discovered, and families were suffering through the closure of losing a loved one. NFL games were canceled, but the players and the owners tried to help with the healing process.

After the season I was united with Trautwig as we did our annual NYPD vs. NYFD football game at Giants Stadium. We did our opening about the two teams, and then Trautwig turned it over to the public-address announcer to do the introduction of the team members. He announced the ones who lost family members in 9/11. The commanding officer presented each family with a framed jersey with their husband's name on the back. The widow and children walked up and accepted the jersey, and each one stood in line waiting for the next one to be announced. I remember looking over at Trautwig with tears in my eyes. We choked up, couldn't say a word, and Trautwig's friendly smile was gone. All I could think about was these kids not having a father as they were growing up, and my heart hurt for every one of them.

America has rebuilt Ground Zero with the Freedom Tower. Time does stop for anyone of us. So slow yourself down and enjoy life. Remember those that lost their lives so we can have freedom.

September 11, 2001, is a day that we should never forget.

Lyons Life Lesson

Fate plays an important part of our lives. Believe in it. Trust it. Things happen for a reason. Value the relationships that you have built and tell the people who are important in your life thank you before it's too late and you find yourself wishing that you had done something or said something before you hear the news that they are no longer with us.

CHAPTER 16
Consistent Playoff Contenders

In 2002, Herm Edwards' second year as the head coach, he tried to improve from a solid 10–6 season record from the year before. There was no doubt that the draft class of 2000 was paying dividends for the organization. John Abraham and Shaun Ellis proved that they were Pro Bowl players, Chad Pennington was getting ready to take over the starting quarterback position, and Anthony Becht was a solid tight end.

Our meetings every Wednesday got better and better as Edwards opened up more about individual players, and what was more valuable for the radio guys was Edwards told us about the Jets' gameplan.

The season, though, didn't open as they had planned. The Jets were 2–5 after the first seven games. This was the season, in which Edwards exploded during a press conference by saying, "You play to win the game!" After that quote things started to change. Pennington took over as the Jets quarterback, and they headed west to play the San Diego Chargers. They were underdogs, but they played inspired. I believe that game, in which they won 44–13, started something special for the remainder of the season. The Jets went on to win seven out of the last nine games, win the AFC East with a record of 9–7, and make the playoffs. Pennington finished the season with 22 touchdowns and only six interceptions. He wasn't born to be a leader, but he developed into one.

Again, the Jets found themselves in a wild–card game, but this time they had a home game against the Indianapolis Colts and Peyton Manning. The stadium was rocking with excitement, and I've never seen the Jets play so inspired, winning 41–0. The Jets defense shut down Manning and limited him to just 137 yards passing and intercepted him twice. With the win they got to move on to the divisional round and once again hit the road and traveled west to play the Oakland Raiders. It was a rematch from the year before where the Jets lost 38–24, but the stakes were higher this time because the winner would move on to the AFC Championship Game. Sadly, the Jets made one too many mistakes, and their season was over after losing to the Raiders once again 30–10.

After back-to-back playoff appearances for Edwards and the Jets, the thought was they just needed a few more pieces to reach a Super Bowl. With the fourth pick in the first round, the Jets drafted Dwayne Robertson, a defensive tackle out of Kentucky. The Jets were hoping with Robertson in the middle and their two defensive ends, Abraham and Ellis, that they would have one of the best defensive lines in the NFL. But Robertson struggled to make the transition from a college player to an NFL player, and his career in the NFL was short-lived.

The key to winning in the NFL, though, is staying healthy. Twenty games in the NFL is a long season. Preseason games back then were a tune up for the season, so the starters could get ready for Opening Day and the team could get its roster set. Also, the fourth game was the most important one as the starters would play most of the game and be ready for the opener that would follow in the week to come. That's not true today. Most NFL starters now sit the fourth game.

The Jets played the New York Giants in that fourth preseason game, and Pennington hurt his hand, causing him to miss the first six games of the 2003 season. Without Pennington the team struggled and lost all of their games in the month of September, going 0–4.

Edwards was the most positive coach that I've ever been around. Every Wednesday we met, and he openly talked about the injuries, the gameplan, and the personnel. But the Jets not only struggled to start the season, but they also lost two out of their last five games in the month of December. In the NFL you must start fast and finish strong, but the Jets went 2–7 in the first and final months. The Jets missed the playoffs for the first time under Edwards and ended the season with a 6–10 record.

The 2004 season represented my fourth year in the booth calling games with Bob Wischusen. Our chemistry was building, and the trust we had with one another continued to enhance the broadcast. I must give credit to our cohosts in the studio, Greg Buttle and Don LaGreca. Every week they were outstanding to work with. Besides being a former player, Buttle has an opinion about everything right or wrong and is going to voice it. His partner, LaGreca, is one of the best in the business. He does the New York Rangers play-by-play during the hockey season and he's not good; he's great. Every afternoon you can hear him on *The Michael Kay Show* on ESPN with Kay and Peter Rosenberg, where he's outstanding in sharing his knowledge of all sports. The chemistry of the three together is an unbelievable listen. LaGreca was a part of our show for 16 years until he became a father of twins and had to step back from the broadcast to spend more time with the twins and his wife, Nancy.

The Jets showed their commitment to Pennington in 2004 by giving him a new contract—a hefty one at that—for seven years and $64.2 million. The money in the NFL is unbelievable, and I was happy for him because he was a hell of a quarterback and a good person.

In the 2004 draft, the Jets drafted wisely and took three players who would make an impact with the Jets and also have long careers in the NFL: Jonathan Vilma, a linebacker out of Miami; Jerricho Cotchery, a wide receiver out of North Carolina State; and Erik Coleman, a safety out of Washington State. There were two question marks going into this season. The media was now wondering about Edwards' clock management and whether Pennington could stay healthy for a 16-game season.

The Jets had been victimized by slow starts the last couple of years, but they started fast in 2004 and won their first five games by playing solid defense and scoring a lot of points. But in Week Nine against the Buffalo Bills, Pennington hurt his shoulder. Nobody knew or would even admit how bad it was. Edwards told us every Wednesday that it was a day-by-day situation. Abraham got hurt late in the year, and as the Jets pushed to make the playoffs, the health of the team was everyone's major concern.

Pennington returned for the end of the year as the Jets closed out the 2004 season with a 10–6 record and another trip to the playoffs under Edwards. Even with a record of 10–6, the Jets were a wild-card team and had to travel west to play San Diego. The Chargers won the AFC West with a 12–4 season and were big favorites to move on to the divisional round. All the Jets could do was play hard and limit their mistakes and maybe, just maybe, they would find a way to win the game.

With a new contact and a banged-up shoulder, Pennington went out and played a solid game, throwing for two touchdowns and almost 300 yards. The defense held a high-powered Chargers offense to just 17 points as the Jets came away with a 20–17 overtime win. The Jets' next game was against the Pittsburgh Steelers, who had a bye week and had won the AFC North with a 15–1 record.

The Pittsburgh game went back and forth after the Jets spotted the Steelers 10 points before they really started to play. Late in the fourth quarter, the Jets had not one but two chances to take the lead, but two missed field goals by Doug Brien sent the game into overtime, and the Steelers kicked a field goal to win 20–17.

I have always believed that one play or two plays in a game—if not executed properly—will cost you a game. Brien missed field goals that could have won the game, but the Jets could have played better in the first quarter, and if they had, maybe it wouldn't have come down to field goals late in the game. Give credit to Edwards and his staff and the players that day for not quitting.

The only mistake that Pennington made that entire season was getting into a no-win media fight with the local beat writers. In December he finally told them that it wasn't their right to cover the team; it was their privilege to cover the team. I never understood why he took that approach with the writers. It's easier to win a football game than it is to beat a writer with a pen and piece of paper. And it was a long offseason for Pennington. After finding out the extent of his shoulder injury, the quarterback underwent surgery to repair a torn rotator cuff and to remove a bone spur in February of 2005.

After missing the two field goals in the playoff loss to the Steelers, the Jets tried to boost their special teams through the 2005 draft by taking kicker Mike Nugent out of Ohio State in the second round. Nugent was another quality person who spent time with the Jets but finished his career with another NFL team. The biggest question was how Pennington bounce would back from his shoulder surgery, and what would happen to Edwards, who was in the final year of his contract.

Edwards was a players' coach. He would never throw publicly one of his players under the bus. But he was more open in our weekly meeting about players, their injuries, their toughness, and their ability to play through pain. Edwards trusted Wischusen and I enough to allow us inside his gameplanning. We knew what we could use in our broadcast and what we couldn't. We never crossed that line.

Even as all the starters and the coaching staff traveled in the first-class section of the plane on away games, Edwards and his wife, Lia, sat in the rear of the plane with the Jets medical staff and the broadcast team. To me that spoke volumes about how Edwards didn't put himself above anyone and was respected by all.

In an offseason move, the Jets traded to bring back one of their own, wide receiver Laveranues Coles, from the Washington Redskins in return for their No. 1 pick from 2001, Santana Moss. I liked Moss, an undersized wide receiver who could also return kicks. But getting back Coles was something that Pennington really wanted. They both were from the same draft class of 2000 and had developed chemistry both on the field and off.

The team struggled in preseason and so did Pennington. Then on September 25 against the Jacksonville Jaguars, Pennington hurt his surgically-repaired shoulder once again. I walked the field with Pennington the next week in Baltimore and talked with him about the business side of the NFL, telling him it was his responsibility to get himself healthy and not to feel compelled to take a pay cut. I respected Pennington as a player, and we had developed a friendship since 2001. So our talk was open and honest.

Calling the game that day with Brooks Bollinger starting at quarterback was challenging. I can't remember how many times he was sacked, but he got hit almost every time he went back to pass. The Jets lost seven games in a row that season from October 16 to December 10 and ended the season 4–12, Edwards' worst record with the Jets.

Edwards took a lot of criticism throughout the season about his time management playing games not to lose. But I don't think it was his fault. It's tough to win when you lose your starting quarterback to injury.

Out in Kansas City, Chiefs head coach Dick Vermeil was getting ready to retire, and the rumor mill was heating up that the Chiefs were looking for a new head coach and that they wanted Edwards. If Edwards left, that meant that once again the Jets would be in a search for a new coach and have no stability at the top of the food chain. The Jets finally worked a deal after the season with Kansas City to trade Edwards for a fourth-round pick in 2006. Kansas City got its guy, and the Jets had to find another new coaching staff once again.

Lyons Life Lesson

Don't make life about your job. Individuals who chase their careers before the other important things like family and friends usually end up with nothing. Don't allow your profession to define who you are. Let your action and your voice define you. I love the New York Jets and the game of football. It's been my life since I started playing football when I was 12 years old, but I will not allow football to define who I am. I want to be remembered for having made a difference in other people's lives, having made the community better, and for being a loving father and husband. The birth of a child is one the most beautiful parts of life. It's God's way of saying this world should continue.

CHAPTER 17
Mangenius and Favre

Starting in 2006, the next three years under Eric Mangini served as an example of why it's so important to be yourself and not to try to be someone else.

I never really got to know Mangini on a professional level or a personal level. He never disrespected me, and I don't recall ever disrespecting him. The one thing that changed was there was no more weekly meeting with Bob Wischusen and I. That was Mangini's choice, not ours. Maybe he had his reasons, but now we were somewhat flying solo when doing the broadcast. Game notes were still provided, but we went from one end of the spectrum with Herm Edwards holding an all-out open meeting on Wednesday to the other end with Mangini.

When Mangini was hired by the Jets, he became the youngest head coach in the NFL. Make no mistake about it. He knew his football and had trained under the best, Bill Belichick. Mangini also put together a heck of staff, bringing in Brian Schottenheimer as his offensive coordinator and promoting the linebackers coach Bob Sutton to be his defensive coordinator. There's a wise idea that if you think you're smart, surround yourself with even smarter people. That's exactly what Mangini did. Mangini also had one of the best special team coordinators in the business in Mike Westhoff, who might even be the best special teams coordinator in the history of the NFL.

The 2006 NFL Draft for the Jets might be the second best draft in team history behind the 2000 draft where they had four first-round draft picks. They focused on where the game is won or lost: the offensive line. In the first round, they drafted D'Brickashaw Ferguson out of Virginia and then selected center Nick Mangold 25 picks later in the first round. As I got to know both Ferguson and Mangold on a personal level, I found out that they weren't just excellent football players. They were people of high character.

Coming off a 4–12 season from the previous year, expectations weren't that high for the 2006 Jets. Even though Mangini was communicating with the media less than I would have liked, he still had the coaching skills to guide the team to the playoffs. It seemed like first-year coaches with the Jets always had the benefit of last year's players, and they went on to make the playoffs. The only exception to this theory was Richie Kotite.

Making a playoff run late in the season when they won five of their last six games proved that Mangini could coach. Three of those wins came on the road, which is hard to do. Making it to the playoffs was one thing. The next step was winning a game or two. In the first round, they matched up against Mangini's old team and the Jets' rival, the New England Patriots. The Jets fell to the Patriots 37–16 in the wild-card game, ending their season.

The 2006 offseason saw a lot of players take pay cuts, a lot of players leave for greener pastures, and a lot of players leave because they weren't needed any more. All of that is life in the NFL. Every year there will be a different team with different players, and no two teams will ever be alike.

This was one of the years when the NFL Hall of Fame should have inducted Joe Klecko. When will they wake up and put him in the Hall? Letters have been written by dozens of members, and Klecko's numbers and accomplishments speak for themselves. The only thing Klecko doesn't have on his resume is a Super Bowl. And trust me that was not his fault. Do the right thing, Canton, and put Joe Klecko in the Hall of Fame where he belongs.

After going 10–6 during Mangini's first year in 2006, everyone expected big things from the Jets, especially owner Woody Johnson. I spent a lot of time before the games talking with Johnson about accountability and his team turning the corner. Johnson really wanted to win for the fans. He spent hours walking the parking lot before home games and talking with them. When Johnson took over ownership of the Jets, he was a fan, but he didn't really know the game inside and out. He, though, quickly adapted to the needs of an NFL team and started to get more involved. In 2006 the stability was rocked at the top when Terry Bradway stepped down as the general manager, and Mike Tannenbaum took over. I liked both Bradway and Tannenbaum. They were good football people, and both were class acts.

The 2007 the Jets drafted Darrelle Revis, a cornerback from Pittsburgh and one of the best players in the history of the Jets organization. Revis was probably one of the best corners the NFL has ever seen. He was so good at matching up one on one with an opposing wide receiver that it earned him the nickname "Revis Island."

People might forget the Jets also drafted David Harris, a linebacker out of Michigan, in the second round that year. Harris had a long career leading the Jets defense and was one of the most underrated players on the defense for years.

This was a new year with new faces and new results. The 2007 Jets took a giant step backward, going 4–12 and losing seven of their first eight games. From the players, to the coaches, to the fans, to the announcers, we all feel the pain when the Jets lose. Wischusen and I are an extension of the team, and nothing is better when the team is playing well and you can talk positive about your team for four quarters. We make it a practice to be honest with our listeners, calling the game as we see it so we can paint an accurate picture. If the Jets thought that changing the announcers would help them win, I would be all for that. I even said that on air. Don't get me wrong: I love what I do, but one day I want to see the Jets holding up that Super Bowl trophy. Whether I'm still announcing the games or not, I would still feel like I'm a part of that accomplishment.

The 2008 season started off with such high hopes because the Jets had two picks in the first round. The last time that happened was in 2006, and they hit pay dirt by drafting two Pro Bowlers in Ferguson and Mangold. This time with the sixth overall pick, they selected Vernon Gholston, a defensive end out of Ohio State, and went to the offensive side late in the first round to draft Dustin Keller, a tight end out of

Purdue. Keller made a smooth transition and became very productive for the Jets and had a nice career in the NFL. But Gholston never turned into the impact player the Jets thought he would be. With his size and speed, he had all the God-given tools to play in the NFL. His body even looked like a Greek god, but the NFL game was so much different from college football and life in the Big Ten, and he just never fulfilled his potential.

This season had so many highs and lows. When the team was in Cleveland for a preseason game, I walked into the lobby of the hotel and saw Chad Pennington walking out of the elevator with his luggage, not thinking much of it. Then I went to my room and got dressed to head to the stadium for the game. I found out that the Jets cut Pennington, and they had acquired Brett Favre from the Green Bay Packers. *Wow, the living legend was going to play for the Jets.* Make no mistake about it: Favre was and still is a legend in the world of NFL football and was inducted into the NFL Hall of Fame.

For everything that Favre had accomplished in his career, he was a quiet guy who kept to himself. Because I was a former player, I think Favre found me easy to talk to. Favre was a fan favorite not only for the Jets, but also the entire league.

Besides the signing of Favre, the Jets also got a Pro Bowler in Alan Faneca from the Pittsburgh Steelers to solidify their offensive line. This team was being built to win now. They also added Damien Woody to the offensive line and Calvin Pace to the defensive side as a much-needed edge rusher.

Players look at the NFL season and divide it into four quarters with four games being played in each quarter. Starting fast and finishing strong doesn't guarantee you a playoff spot, but more than likely, it will help you get there. With new faces and a legend at quarterback, the Jets started off with a victory against the Miami Dolphins and their old starting quarterback, Pennington. At the end of the first quarter, the Jets were 2–2 despite all of their new parts. All was good in Jets land.

Good, solid football in the second quarter of the season had the Jets looking strong at the midseason point at 5–3. In the third quarter, the Jets were kicking into high gear, going 3–1 over that time frame, and were heading into the home stretch with an 8–4 record. In Week 14 they went to San Francisco to play the 49ers and lost, making their record 8–5. They came back the next week to Giants Stadium and beat the Buffalo Bills 31–27, giving them a 9–5 record with two games left on the schedule. They were in a sweet spot in the AFC East, but it seemed like something was wrong—not just with the team but with their quarterback. In fact, after the Jets reached 8–3, they lost three of their next four games, and Favre's numbers told the story. He had one touchdown pass and six interceptions the rest of the way.

Anyhow that 9–5 team headed to the west coast to play the Seattle Seahawks, a team that was struggling and really had nothing to play for. This is the game where the wheels fell off.

It was a miserable day with rain and snow. I interviewed Warren Moon before the game about the two teams, and we talked about the durability of Favre. The Jets received the open kickoff and started at their own 20-yard line. They came out ready to play, moving the ball right down the field all the way to the 2-yard line and then they found themselves in a fourth-down situation with a half a yard to pick up a first down. They had taken almost seven minutes off the clock on this 13-play drive. I was in the booth, saying the Jets had to go for it by running behind their Pro Bowl guard, Faneca, and Pro Bowl center, Mangold, but not Mangini, who elected to kick a field goal. *Are you kidding me? You need to win this game.* Even if they hadn't picked up the first down, they would have had Seattle backed up at its own 2-yard line. Instead the game played out so that the Jets never got inside Seattle's red zone the remainder of the game.

The Jets lost the game 13–3, and the loss was clearly on Mangini and the coaching staff. This was the drive chart for the Jets in the second half: punt, punt, punt, turn over on downs, and interception. That just shows there was not a lot of adjustment at halftime to deal with the weather. It seemed like the Jets couldn't do anything right in the second half. Life is like football. It's about making the right choices and taking advantages of opportunities. The Jets missed out on their opening drive by not going for it on fourth and a half a yard. To make matters worse, at the end of the game, I was walking across the end zone to get to the tunnel by the Jets locker room when I got hit by a snowball in the head from some-one in the crowd. There were hundreds of snowballs being thrown. They really weren't snowballs. They were ice balls. It sounds funny now, but it wasn't back then.

The Jets were then in a must-win situation with one game to go against Pennington and the Dolphins. Win and you're in. Lose and you need help. They lost 24 17, ending their season. What killed the Jets is that they went 1–3 in the final quarter of the season. The Jets had seven players voted to the Pro Bowl team that season but didn't make the play-offs. I still remember that Seattle game, and it still bothers me to this day.

During December of 2008, I lost someone that was very special to me, a 15-year-old girl named Lauren. She was 10 years old when she got diagnosed with Chordoma tumor, a rare type of cancer that occurs in the bones of the base of the skull and spine.

She had a beautiful smile and eyes that lifted your soul. She loved poetry so her wish for the foundation was to have all her poems published in a book. With the help of one of our volunteer's, Gary Lake, we were able to publish an inspirational book called *Black and Brown Makers*.

Lauren got an invitation to attend the White House and read her poem to President Bush's wife. My son, Jesse, and I got to see it in per-son.

Then her cancer got very aggressive. The foundation was hosting our annual Christmas party, and Lauren showed up in her wheelchair. Her smile was gone, her body was fragile, and we both knew her time was near. I bent over to hug and kiss her on the forehead and told her how much I loved her. She was tired. She had given cancer a great fight, but in the end, the cancer won the battle.

Lauren passed away a few days later on December 20, and my daughter, Megan, and I went to a small town in New Jersey for the wake and the funeral. It was raining, sleeting, and snowing when we reached the funeral home for the wake. People were lined up out the door to pay their respect to Lauren.

As we attended the funeral the next day, Lauren gave me a message through her eulogy that would change my life. The priest who delivered the eulogy was spot on as he welcomed everyone to celebrate the life of Lauren. "I've been a part of this parish for the past 15 years," the priest said. "I was here when Lauren was baptized, I was here when Lauren received her first holy communion, and I was here when she received her confirmation, and now I'm here to celebrate her life as she enters the kingdom of heaven. Lauren used to take a walk with God every single day of her life. Some days she would take a long walk. Some days it was a short walk, but every single day she took that walk. Until one day she took that walk, and she got tired and looked up to the Good Lord and said, 'I'm tired. Can we go home?' And the Good Lord looked back at Lauren and replied, 'We're closer to my house than we are to yours, and if you go to mine, you'll be free of all your pain and live with me forever.' Lauren wants to know how far do you walk. If you don't walk at all, start walking. If you think you're walking far enough every day, walk a little further because there will come a time in everyone's life that you're closer to His house rather the yours."

CHAPTER 18
Rex, The Sanchize, and AFC Championship Games

History once again repeated itself. After a frustrating season for the Jets in 2008, the coaching staff was fired, and a new one was hired. This was also the last season in Giants Stadium. The new coaching staff had personality like none other than I've been around, and that started with the head coach Rex Ryan, who was outspoken, funny, and he could coach and motivate like no one else. To help Ryan impart his message, the Jets brought in two of his former Baltimore Ravens players—Bart Scott and Jim Leonhard—to help on the field and in the locker room. Ryan was also a breath of fresh air for the media. We went from a one-word answers from Eric Mangini to a colorful story from Ryan.

I enjoyed Ryan. He talked old school and coached old school. He reminded me of Walt Michaels because they both were cut from the same mold. I've always believed if Michaels wasn't fired after we lost to the Miami Dolphins in the "Mud Bowl" in 1983, we would have won the Super Bowl sometime in the 1980s. That was Ryan's gameplan: to win a Super Bowl and not kiss anyone's rings along the way. He made that statement in reference to playing in the same division as Bill Belichick and the New England Patriots. Ryan was now the face and the voice of the New York Jets organization, but he put together a heck of a coaching staff starting with the assistant head coach Bill Callahan, who also coached the offensive line and was known in the NFL as being one of the best at that position. The offensive coordinator was Brian Schottenheimer, who also was known for calling a solid game. Anthony Lynn coached the running backs, and Mike Devlin assisted the offensive line. Defensively, the coordinator was Mike Pettine, who Ryan had worked with in Baltimore, and the secondary coach was Dennis Thurman.

From Day One when I introduced myself to Ryan, it was a friendship that was already established. I knew it was going to be fun working with him. You could ask him any question. You might not like the answer, but Ryan was a straight shooter.

Rex Ryan was an old-school coach, but he was also outspoken, funny, and a great motivator. (New York Jets)

The Jets wheeled and dealed in the offseason, trading picks and players, and when all was said and done, that left them with only three picks in the upcoming draft. And with only three picks, you better be right, or you'll set the organization back for decades. With one of those three picks, they selected Mark Sanchez, a quarterback out of USC. Think about the deal the Jets had to make to get him. They traded their first and second-round picks and players to the Cleveland Browns for their first-round pick, which was the fifth pick in the first round. That was a huge gamble. In the third round, they drafted running back Shonn Greene out of Iowa. With their final pick in the sixth round, they drafted Matt Slauson, a guard out of Nebraska. It seemed like the Jets were banking of Sanchez to be their franchise quarterback, even though the USC head coach Pete Carroll stated that he didn't feel Sanchez was ready for the NFL. The Jets made a huge investment in Sanchez. They not only moved up to get him fifth overall, but they also gave him a five-year contract worth $50 million, including $28 million guaranteed. With that type of commitment from the Jets, you knew who the starting quarterback was going to be on Opening Day.

Sanchez didn't come into camp as a cocky kid from California. He was smart, humble, and eager to learn. The best thing going for Sanchez was that the face of the organization wasn't the young quarterback. It was their head coach, Rex Ryan.

He believed in old-school football—ground and pound—and he had the horses upfront on the offensive line to do so. If they limited the mistakes of a rookie quarterback, they had a chance of making the playoffs. During the mid-season point, Ryan told me that that once the team got inside the red zone that he told Sanchez to think of red lights and green lights when throwing the ball. Green light was when you're 100 percent sure of a completion, and a red light meant don't throw it because there's some doubt. Live for another play, take the field goal, and put three points on the board.

Everyone, including the entire organization, his coaches, his players, the media, and the fans, bought into Ryan. He was unpredictable, fun, charming, and stood up for his players. With everyone riding the Ryan bus, the Jets started off with a 3–1 record in the first quarter of the season, and Sanchez was holding his own as the starting quarterback. The middle part of the season was a learning curve for everyone except Bob Wischusen and I in the radio booth. We've seen this before where the Jets lose five out of their next six games and go onto their final six games with a record of 4–6.

We were about to see just how good Ryan was and whether he could pull this team together or if it had hit that imaginary wall. Ryan went back to the basics. The Jets ran the ball, won the battle up front, and won five out of their next six games to finish 9–7 and earn a wild-card spot in the playoffs despite having Sanchez complete only 12 touchdowns passes while throwing 20 interceptions. It was playoff time for a rookie head coach and a rookie quarterback, but they took their show on the road. Sometimes playing on the road is good for a young team because you don't have any distractions like buying tickets, going out with friends the night before a game, etc. Instead everything was planned out for you.

The first stop was Cincinnati, and the Jets had beaten the Bengals in Week 17 of the regular season 37–0. The Jets ended up beating Cincinnati in back-to-back weeks, winning the wild-card game 24–14. The next stop was playing in San Diego against the Chargers, who were the No. 2 seed in the conference playoff. But confidence for the Jets was at an all-time high as the team headed west a day early to get used to the climate and the time difference. In the playoffs it didn't matter how much you won by. What mattered was winning. The Jets trailed at halftime 7–0 but put 17 points up in the second half to pick up their second win in the playoffs of 2009. This time it was a 17–14 score. For only the third time since I join the organization in 1979, the Jets were heading to an AFC Championship Game. This time it was against Indianapolis

Colts and Peyton Manning. The Jets beat the Colts in the regular season in Week 16 at Lucas Oil Stadium, so the team was very familiar with the setting. The Jets also knew very well what Manning could do to them if they didn't play solid football for 60 minutes.

After a scoreless first quarter, the Colts struck first with a field goal, but the Jets answered right back with a long, 80-yard completion from Sanchez to Braylon Edwards that went for a touchdown. Edwards was a good guy, and I was happy to see him enjoying his moment of greatness. At halftime the Jets were on top of the Colts 17–13. All I could think about was if they played solid defense and didn't turn the ball over, the Jets were going to the Super Bowl. But the Colts scored 17 unanswered points in the second half, and the season was over after the Jets lost 30–17.

I stood with Ryan outside the buses after the game. I told him how great a run the Jets had, and then Manning walked up to congratulate Ryan on an outstanding season, and Ryan offered his congratulations to Manning on his victory and wished him good luck in the Super Bowl. What I witnessed that day were two individuals with a great deal of respect for each other.

After the 2019 run the Jets had to the AFC Championship Game, HBO's *Hard Knocks* came knocking on their door. At that time who wouldn't want 24 hours of nonstop Ryan? As much as Ryan loved the camera, the camera loved him. The team was training at Cortland University, and the setting couldn't get any better because Ryan was in your living room every week. I didn't watch many of the episodes on the Jets, but I do remember laughing hard after I watched cornerback Antonio Cromartie try to name his nine children. That was totally hilarious.

Because Ryan's rookie season was so unbelievable, people around the league started to take notice and wanted more of the Jets and more of Ryan. The Jets made a lot of moves in the offseason, and there were plenty of veteran players who wanted to come to New York. Two future Hall of Famers, LaDainian Tomlinson and Jason Taylor, signed along with veteran quarterback Mark Brunell. The Jets also picked up two veterans by trade: Cromartie and Santonio Holmes.

The NFL draft brought Kyle Wilson, a cornerback, in the first round, and an offensive lineman in the second named Vladimir Ducasse, but both had short-lived careers with the Jets. They also took Joe McKnight, a running back out of USC, and their final pick in the fifth round was John Conner, a fullback out of Kentucky. So in the first two drafts under Ryan and Mike Tannenbaum, the Jets had a total of seven picks. When you have only seven picks in two years, you better hit on five of the seven or you'll find yourself on a sinking ship without a life jacket.

Along with their appearance on national television for *Hard Knocks*, they started their journey of the 2010 season with another promise of a Super Bowl appearance, a new stadium, new faces, and more pressure on the players every time Ryan spoke.

But the 2010 Jets responded with a 11–5 record that season and they didn't lose a road game until Week 13 against the Patriots when they lost 45–3. It was a game, in which the Jets simply didn't show up. They were outplayed and outcoached, but it was just one game and a game that they could learn from. What really killed the Jets was that after going 9–2 in their first 11 games they only won two of their next five games. That's not the way they wanted to close out the season. It's hard to believe that finishing 11–5 would place you as the sixth seed in the playoffs that year. But the Patriots finished 14–2, including a Week Two, 28–14 loss to the Jets. Not winning their division meant it was once again time for the Jets to hit the road, and the first stop was the wild-card game against the Colts. It was revenge time since the Colts and Manning kept them from going to the Super Bowl in 2009.

This Colts game was different from the previous year's game because Ryan made adjustments and turned the game into a defensive fistfight. As a result, the Jets came out on top with a 17–16 victory. The defense held Manning to just one touchdown pass and limited the Colts to just three field goals in the second half. The next stop for the Jets was another trip back to face Tom Brady in Foxboro, Massachusetts.

The Jets proved in Week Two that they could stand toe to toe with New England when they won by 14 points, but they also knew in the back of their mind what happened later in the season when they lost by 42. Brady may be the best player to play the quarterback position ever. But you can take the best and make them look ordinary by putting them on their back. That's exactly what Ryan wanted to do. His gameplan was to blitz Brady from every angle: right side, left side, up the middle. He was throwing the kitchen sink at Brady every passing play. It worked. They sacked Brady five times that game and won 28–21. It was also the game where Scott was asked about going to Pittsburgh to play the Steelers in the AFC Championship Game in the next round, and he responded by famously barking out: "Can't Wait!" Scott wasn't just talking about himself, but the team leader was talking for the entire team. This team was on a mission and trying their best to keep a promise that their head coach made before the season that the Jets were going to the Super Bowl. Now they were just one game away.

The AFC Championship Game in Pittsburgh meant a homecoming for Holmes, the MVP of the Super Bowl for the Steelers back in 2008. To beat the Steelers, you must play for four quarters and limit your mistakes. Beside Seattle, the Pittsburgh crowd may have the loudest fans. Once they start waving those towels, they are hard to control. In the first half, the Jets were terrible—almost like they weren't ready to play because they were trailing the Steelers at the half 24–3. When you go into a locker room at halftime trailing, someone must stand up and hold the team accountable. Someone needs to light a fire under the players asses to turn the second half into game. Most of all, Ryan and his coaching staff had to make adjustments because the difference between being good and great are the adjustments you make to get your team back in the game. The Jets came out in the second half and looked like a completely different team. They shut out the Steelers, but not being able to score on their last drive left them five points short, and they lost 24–19.

After back-to-back AFC Championship Game losses, the other teams were asking if the Jets could take the next step. Well, in those first two seasons, Ryan was certainly the real deal, and the New York Jets band-wagon was growing and growing. He made covering the Jets fun again.

For those years broadcasting them, the radio crew had a tradition in the playoffs. The crew consisted of Joe Loughran, Dave Shapiro, Richie Providence, Mike Altieri, Wischusen, Bobby Parente, Gary Jefferies, and Al Pereira. It started off in 2009 at the wild-card game when we went for a steak dinner, and I dropped some steak sauce on my new white shirt. At the time I didn't think anything of it, but after the Jets won, Loughran, who was being very superstitious about everything, thought we should do the same routine the following week. So we did. After a good steak dinner, I once again spilled steak sauce on my same white shirt except this time Loughran thought it would be added luck if everyone spilled something on my shirt. My shirt ended up looking like a palette. I had food everywhere, but the Jets won.

Dinner before the AFC Championship Game was wild. It was like a cafeteria food fight. Food was thrown in my direction by everyone, including Jets fans sitting at nearby tables. Before the AFC Championship Game, my shirt looked like a crime scene. If the Jets had won the AFC Championship Game, I was ready to go to the Super Bowl dinner in a shower curtain.

If the Jets get back to the playoffs, I'm sure the tradition will continue and I'll be more than happy to supply a new white shirt.

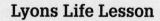

Lyons Life Lesson

Every day of our life, hundreds of families hear sad news about a loved one. How an individual reacts will be a testament to their faith. Our faith will be questioned by the words we speak, our actions, and how we live our life. When all is said and done, faith will carry us from a dark place in our lives to a brighter tomorrow. As hard as it may seem, never lose faith.

CHAPTER 19
Santonio Holmes

As the 2011 Jets hoped to win one more playoff game to reach the greatest stage, I reached the highest level personally. It was such an honor just to be on the College Football Hall of Fame ballot, but to get the phone call that I was elected was breathtaking. That class included players like Deion Sanders, Eddie George, Doug English, Russell Maryland, Jake Scott, Carlos Alvarez, Will Shields, Sandy Stephens, Gene Washington, Rob Waldrop, Darryl Talley, and the great coach of Michigan, Lloyd Carr.

When I got the call, I hung up the phone with tears in my eyes. Calling my wife, Christine, and then calling other family members was a humbling experience and honor. I would be representing the University of Alabama, my teammates, the fans, and Bear Bryant in the class of 2011. I can't tell you the feeling of accomplishment I felt that day. Here I was, just a kid from Pinellas Park, Florida, one of seven children, going to the College Football Hall of Fame. I reflected on my high school teammates, guys like Ted LaVenture, Tim Ginty, and Joe Ezzo, who sacrificed just as much as I did back then. They were a part of this journey. They were a part of this honor. How could I ever say thank you to my high school head football coach, George O'Brien, who saw more in me back than then I saw in myself, for what he meant in my life? My family had always supported me, and this was also their moment. For my brother, Dan, who stopped me from quitting football back in 1972, it was totally surreal.

On the NFL side, the Jets may have lost back-to-back AFC Championship Games, but they were moving in the right direction. Rex Ryan kept talking, bringing more excitement to the team while also putting more pressure on his players. Opposing teams didn't want to beat the Jets. They wanted to beat Ryan.

The 2011 draft brought some talented players to the Jets, starting with their first pick, Muhammad Wilkerson, a defensive lineman from Temple, the same college that produced Joe Klecko three decades earlier. The Jets

During an emotional night, the Jets opened their 2011 season against the Dallas Cowboys at home on *Monday Night Football* on the 10th anniversary of 9/11. (New York Jets)

also drafted Bilal Powell, a running back out of Louisville who proved to be a valuable asset for years to come. Jeremy Kerley, a talented wide receiver from TCU, was drafted in the fifth round and became a safety blanket for quarterbacks. Speaking of quarterbacks, the Jets picked Greg McElroy out of my alma mater, Alabama, in the seventh round. Ryan's job was to blend these draft choices with the free agents they brought in and his players from the year before and make another at the AFC Championship Game—only to win it this time.

The opening game was very emotional. The Jets opened their season against the Dallas Cowboys at home on *Monday Night Football* on the 10th anniversary of 9/11. The American flag was flying high as it was stretched from end zone to end zone, covering the entire field, and the moment of silence seemed like it lasted forever as those who were lost that day were once again remembered.

The game had multiple storylines. It was Mark Sanchez vs. Tony Romo; Rex vs. his twin brother, Rob, who was coaching in Dallas; and, of course, you had America's team, the Dallas Cowboys, vs. the New York Jets. The Jets fell behind in the first quarter 7–0 and struggled with four punts on their first four possessions, but right before halftime, Sanchez connected with tight end Dustin Keller for a touchdown to cut the score to 10–7 as the players went into the locker room. One thing I knew in my first two years of working with Ryan was that he had the ability to motivate his players, and he was going to make his halftime speech powerful. The second half was going to be different.

At the end of the third quarter, the Jets were trailing 17–10. This was a good, hard-nosed football game that came down to the fourth quarter. The Jets defense came up big, creating three turnovers, and the offense put up 17 points. As a result, the Jets came from behind to win 27–24. Ryan was the man; it seemed the more he talked, the better his team responded.

As the first quarter of the season closed, the Jets were 2–2, and at the halfway point of the season, they were 5–3. Record-wise, they were looking pretty good except it seemed like a handful of players were unhappy about how many touches they were getting per game. The attitude seemed to change from a team concept to an individual attitude. The media wanted to know whether Ryan was losing the locker room. But from meeting with Ryan and talking with him, that just didn't seem to be the case. He seemed to have the pulse of his entire team.

The Jets headed into their final three games with a 8–5 record and they looked to make it to the playoffs for the third straight year, but they had to face two NFC East teams, the Philadelphia Eagles and New York Giants, and close out the season against the Miami Dolphins on the road. The Eagles game was a disaster, a 45–19 loss. The Giants game was a battle, but one play broke the spirit of the Jets and their fans. As the second quarter of the game was coming to a close and the Giants had the ball at their own one-yard line, the Jets defense had a total meltdown and allowed a 99-yard completion from Eli Manning to Victor Cruz for a touchdown. That play should have been a completion of 10 to 15 yards but not a touchdown. The

Jets never recovered and lost 29–14, dropping their overall record to 8–7. Their playoff hopes were slipping away.

When the Jets play the Dolphins, you can throw out their record. These two franchise don't like each other—plain and simple. The Jets had the firepower to beat the Dolphins. What they had to do was not beat themselves. In the fourth quarter, Bob Wischusen and I noticed something going on in the Jets offensive huddle, a little disagreement of sort, between Santonio Holmes and one of the offensive linemen. Then it happened. Holmes walked out of the huddle to the bench and took his helmet off. Holmes had taken himself out of the game. As a former player, all I could think was, *Are you kidding me?* I couldn't believe one of the most valuable players on the offensive side of the ball was taking himself out of the game. Holmes didn't play the remainder of the game, and the Jets lost their third straight game to end the season at 8–8 and miss the playoffs.

Holmes benching himself showed the lack of respect he had for his team, his teammates, and himself. That single move was the worst I have ever seen in my 40-plus years with the Jets. I admit I don't know fully what happened in the huddle between the players involved, but benching yourself was totally unacceptable. To make matters worse, Holmes was one of the team captains. That move didn't just hurt the team's chances of winning, but it also put Ryan in an awkward position.

Holmes was an incredible talent on the football field. Who could forget that he was a Super Bowl MVP when the Pittsburgh Steelers won Super Bowl XLIII? But you could tell something was off when the Steelers traded him to the Jets in April of 2010 for just a fifth-round pick in the upcoming draft. Sure, Holmes had his problems off the field, but his talent on the field could help any NFL team win. Ryan was willing to take anyone's problem and try to fix it.

One of the responsibilities that Wischusen and I have for the radio team is going into the locker room after every game and getting interviews with the players. I know how difficult it is as a player to have the media ask questions after a loss, but Wischusen and I are an extension of the team. We're not going to ask a question that will put the player in a bad position with the organization or their teammates. Joe Loughran, the radio producer, always liked to get different players in the locker room, and one of those players was Holmes. I went up to Holmes every week and asked if I could ask him one question for Jets radio, and the answer was always the same. "No, bro. Not today," he said.

Week after week the fans wanted to hear from Holmes, and I couldn't get an interview. Maybe it was me. Over the years there's been a lot of stand-up guys in the Jets locker room who I could get win or lose, but to help our postgame broadcast, you wanted to get the stars of the game, and Holmes was one of those players.

I was sitting in my office one day when the phone rang, and it was Holmes' attorney. He asked me to attend a charity event that Holmes was hosting to benefit children with autism. My first thought was, *Really? This guy snubs me every game in the locker room and he wants me to attend his event.* After explaining my position to his attorney, he said he would talk to Holmes and resolve that issue.

When I went to the event that following Monday, I saw a different Holmes than the one I saw on the field. He came up to me and thanked me for attending his event, gave me a man hug, and told me he would do an interview after the next game whether the Jets won or lost. That night was special for the children with autism and their families, Holmes was engaging and warm, and his current teammates were very supportive.

When Sunday came around, I told Loughran in our production meeting that Holmes had agreed to do an interview after the game. I told him that we should be ready in the locker room so I could get in and out of the interview without taking up too much of his time. Well, the Jets lost the game, I went to do my interview with Ryan and then headed to the locker room. We were all set for the Holmes interview. Dave Shapiro met me at the door, and we headed over to Holmes' locker where he was sitting alone. I walked up to Holmes and asked if we could get a couple of questions, and to my surprise, he said, "No, bro. Not today."

What? What happened to the man hug on Monday and the commitment to do the interview? I was floored, and if my microphone was live, the listening audience probably would have heard me say, "You son of a bitch, you used me for a charity event, and this is how you're going to treat me."

Granted I would have attended the event anyway in honor of a good friend of mine who has a son with autism, but come on, Holmes. Be a man of your word. Whether it's right or wrong, I can honestly say I never looked at Holmes the same way. He could have been the greatest player on the field at his position, and there were games in which he was, but as a man, I just didn't respect him. Maybe that's why the Steelers only asked for a fifth-round pick for a Super Bowl MVP. I guess that's where the old saying "a leopard never changes his spots" comes in. Or maybe it was just me being old school.

CHAPTER 20
The Butt Fumble

Going into his fourth year as the head coach of the Jets, Rex Ryan had his hands full, and there was plenty of noise. The offense struggled in 2011, scoring 281 points, which was 30th in the NFL. The defense ranked eighth in the NFL, but you need points to win in the NFL. The other problem Ryan had to deal with was that he had players who were unhappy with the offensive scheme. The wide receivers wanted the ball more, the running backs wanted more touches, and he had to be more hands-on with the offensive gameplan. So his first move was firing the offensive coordinator Brian Schottenheimer and hiring Tony Sparano. The question was what would this do to the development of Mark Sanchez. The quarterback had managed the game well enough to take the Jets to back-to-back AFC Championship Games in his first two seasons in the NFL and was looking to rebound from the year he had in 2011. The Jets believed in Sanchez so much that they gave him a contract extension in March of 2012 that included $20 million in guaranteed money.

The offseason chatter about Sanchez was brutal. Teammates talked about his lack of commitment to the game and toward the team. That was a very strong statement made by some of his teammates who didn't have the self-respect to put their names to those quotes. I'm not even sure those quotes were made by teammates. It could've just been a beat writer stirring the pot. Either way Ryan had a lot on his plate.

The draft was shaky at best. The Jets took Quinton Coples, a defensive lineman out of North Carolina, in the first round and in second round they took Stephen Hill, a wide receiver out of Georgia Tech. Neither player had an impact on the Jets roster. You can't afford to miss on those picks. They don't just hurt the franchise today, but they cripple you for years in the future.

In a surprising move the Jets also acquired Tim Tebow from the Denver Broncos maybe because he was a big name. Tebow is one of the finest individuals I have ever met. He's nothing short of a class act.

In a year's time, quarterback Mark Sanchez went from meeting President Bush before a game to getting benched after throwing four interceptions in a game. (New York Jets)

I met Tebow for the first time in Cincinnati. As I walked up to introduce myself to him, I extended my right hand and said, "Marty Lyons, University of Alabama 1978, glad to meet you. How about a Roll Tide?"

Tebow looked at me and smiled. "I wish I could, but being a University of Florida Gator, I can't," he said. Say what you want about his quarterback ability in the NFL, but he's another individual who wasn't defined by his football career.

Preseason for the Jets was terrible as they went 0–4. Nobody puts a lot a merit on those games except the fans, but red flags were waving as the offense struggled to find the end zone, scoring only 31 points while Ryan's defense allowed 88 points. The defense was always Ryan's baby. He was always an attack mode and emphasizing getting the quarterback on the ground. His offense was simple: ground and pound and win it up front with the guys in the trenches.

Sanchez struggled in 2012 as the offense tried to change their identity from a ground-and-pound team to a passing offense. Sanchez had games where he was missing wide-open receivers, and his pass completion was down to a 50 percent completion rating. As poorly as he was playing going into the month of December, the Jets still had a chance with a 6–7 record. As we have seen many times over the years, the Jets couldn't close out the season on a winning note, losing their final three games. They ended the season without a playoff berth for a second consecutive year and had a 6–10 record. Despite having a new contract, Sanchez's final numbers for the year were 13 touchdowns and 18 interceptions. He was also benched for Greg McElroy toward the end of the season after throwing four interceptions against the Tennessee Titans.

As if the season couldn't get any worse, an embarrassing play happened on Thanksgiving eve on national television when the Jets were hosting the New England Patriots. Sanchez went back to pass. With the pocket collapsing around him, he put his head down and ran into the backside of one of his offensive linemen and fumbled the ball. The play would live on in infamy as "the butt fumble." As I watched the play live, Sanchez's first mistake was missing the handoff to the running back. His second mistake was not securing the ball. I'm not sure who made the mistake in the backfield. Sanchez was just trying to make something out of a broken play. The Patriots picked up the fumble and returned it for a touchdown, which just magnified the play. That play shouldn't define Sanchez's career with the Jets. But in so many circles, it does, which isn't fair.

Everyone must remember: you win as a team and you lose as a team. Stability starts with the coaching staff and the front office. Ryan had to get back to his winning ways, or people would forget about those two AFC Championship Game appearances and he would be on the cutting block.

Ryan really was a good guy though, which he demonstrated during his interactions with a boy named Tyler. A friend of mine knew of a kid who was refusing more hospital treatments. I have been down this road many times with foundation kids. Treatments, surgeries, and the four walls of the hospital will take their toll on you, especially on a child.

So I grabbed a football and headed to the hospital. Tyler was laying in the bed with a feeding tube. I talked with him about not giving up, about fighting, about how much his family and friends loved him. The common bond we had was football. Tyler loved football and he loved the Jets. So, I made him a deal. If he started back on his treatment, I'd take him and his father to a Jets game. His eyes lit up. He had never been to a game.

The Jets were 100 percent behind my promise to Tyler. They got him tickets and field passes for him and his father. We walked the field, and I introduced Tyler to players and to Ryan, who was the best. He spent time talking with Tyler and making him feel special. This wasn't the first time that Ryan extended himself to one of the foundation's wish children nor was it the first time the Jets were supportive. I've lost count of how my times I've been able to offer an invite to a game or an autographed picture from a Jets player to help a child through a difficult time. The Jets have always said yes, and, most importantly, Tyler is still fighting today.

I met another boy named Matt when he was around 3 years old who had a brain tumor. When he wasn't in the hospital, he had to spend most of the time at his grandmother's house, and the backyard was just a bed of wood chips with an old rusty swing set.

The grandmother asked if there was anything I could do to renovate the backyard. Mike Ryan, the owner of Landtek, where I've worked for about two decades, gave me the green light to install a new synthetic turf in the backyard free of charge.

The construction period took an extra couple of weeks due to the depth of the wood chips. After we completed the turf, I reached out to friends of mine at American Recreational owned by Bobby and Kevin Brown and asked them for help. Within a week we had a new swing set free of charge. The acts of kindness shown by so many people were unbelievable. While all this work was being completed at the grandmother's house, Matt was with his family in Boston preparing for surgery. Just prior to the surgery, the doctors called for another MRI to make sure the tumor was still in the same location and didn't grow over the weekend. To their surprise the tumor was gone. Divine intervention. All the prayers for Matt must have been answered. As a believer in faith, I witnessed a true miracle.

Matt has been cancer free for over 10 years now. Do you believe in miracles? I do.

*　*　*

The offseason after the 2012 season saw drastic changes. The Jets fired their general manager Mike Tannenbaum and hired John Idzik. Mike Westhoff, the best special teams coach in the business, retired. Ryan lost other members of his coaching staff. The Jets started off with a new offensive coordinator when they fired Tony Sparano and hired Marty Mornhinweg. Three offensive coordinators in three years is never good for quarterback development. Stability starts at the top, and like a tall tree on a windy day, the Jets front office and coaching staff were like branches snapping and hitting the ground.

The Jets had two first-round picks in the draft and they went on the defensive side of the ball, taking Dee Milliner, a cornerback out of Alabama, with the ninth overall pick and Sheldon Richardson, a defensive tackle out of Missouri, with the 13th pick. They also drafted Geno Smith, a quarterback out of West Virginia, in the second round, but probably their best pick came in the third round when they selected Brian Winters, a guard out of Kent State.

I got to know this draft class well because Dave Szott, a former offensive lineman and the player development director for the Jets, asked me to address the class and explain to them what it takes to be a professional athlete and what they could expect playing in New York. Smith was there with his mother, and I gave them both my cell number in case of an emergency. I also spent time with Richardson. I could tell he was a good guy but that he also would need some guidance.

While the draft choice looked promising on paper, Milliner couldn't stay healthy and had a short career with the Jets. Richardson went on to win the AFC Rookie of the Year award with an outstanding season. He should have been able to build on that rookie season, but he got into trouble both on and off the field and was traded to the Seattle Seahawks years later. He had the athletic ability to be one of the best defensive linemen in the league, but he had to be pointed in the right direction, something that he found hard to do. Winters developed into an outstanding guard, winning a starting position with skills he still has today. Winters is a perfect example of hard work and dedication paying off.

One of the craziest moves Rex Ryan ever made as a head coach happened in their third preseason game that year. Playing against the New York Giants in the third quarter, he put his starting quarterback back in the game, stating he wanted to win the game. Well, they won the game in overtime, but they lost their starting quarterback, Mark Sanchez, for the season with a shoulder injury. That was one of the decisions that Ryan made that I could never understand. It was a preseason game. I don't care if it was the Giants with whom you share the stadium. Taking your quarterback out of the game for health reasons and then reinserting him into a game that doesn't count in the standings was a bad move. As a result, the Jets had to start the season with Smith, a rookie quarterback.

Smith had some talent. He could spin the ball and he was smart. But adjusting to the speed of the game, controlling the huddle, and earning the respect of his teammates is challenging for any rookie.

As the season played out, Smith took his hits and was sacked 43 times. He ended up throwing 21 interceptions while only throwing 12 touchdowns and completing 56 percent of his passes. The team was still able to ground and pound with Chris Ivory and Bilal Powell, but the team went 8–8 and once again missed the playoffs.

While the Jets had a disappointing season, I received a great honor from the team in 2013. The Jets put me into their Ring of Honor during halftime of a Week Six game. When the announcement was made during a preseason game by Bob Wischusen, I was brought to tears. I never thought about the honor even while I saw some of my former teammates get inducted. I never thought that my name would be considered. So it was a total surprise to me to join the likes of Joe Namath, Joe Klecko, Al Toon, Wesley Walker, and Mark Gastineau.

The Jets made the weeks leading up to the Week Six game against the Pittsburgh Steelers so exciting for me and my family. Bob Parente and Chris Pierce from the Jets did more than I could ever ask for. On the day of the induction, my wife told me one thing before I left the hotel room: don't cry. I was thinking, *How could I not cry? This was an honor that would last a lifetime.*

As I walked on the field at halftime and saw my family and friends all wearing my No. 93 jerseys, I started to get choked up. I felt my emotions taking over my body, but then I saw two familiar faces who calmed me down. First, I saw Al Trautwig. He ushered me into the business of broadcasting while doing the *Jets Journal* show. He had a way with words, making me smile and forgetting the nerves that I felt. The second person I saw was Joe Mondello, the chairman of the Republican Party in Nassau County. Mondello and I became good friends, and he was like a father to me. He was actually the one person who pushed me to go back to college and get my degree. My high school coach, George O'Brien, and my high school teammates, Ted LaVenture and Tim Ginty, were there to share the moment as well.

As I was thanking everyone from past Jets personnel to current players to past teammates and the fans, I wanted to thank the children from the foundation. I stated that this honor was more about them than it was about me. Those children who had survived their illness taught me how to fight and never give up. This honor also helped remember the poor kids who did not survive. At the end of my speech, I thanked the fans for their support, respect, and love they had shown me since the day I was drafted back in 1979.

My entire family was there that day to celebrate that moment, and at the end of my speech, my oldest son handed me his daughter, Liv, and I held her up while she clapped. That moment with Liv wasn't planned. It just happened and capped off one of the greatest honors I ever received.

Lyons Life Lesson

A commitment is taking the words of a promise and making them become a reality. When you don't think you have the time, you find time because of that commitment. When there's someone who needs to talk to you, you're there and you don't ask for something in return. Commitment is a word we should all have in our vocabulary.

CHAPTER 21
The Todd Bowles Era

By the beginning of the 2014 season, the back-to-back years of the AFC Championship Games lived in the distant past for Rex Ryan. The NFL game is what have you done for me lately, and going 8–8 in 2013 wasn't good enough.

The Jets personnel and coaching staff looked like they were stuck in a revolving door. Players left, coaches left, and then players came in on Tuesday for a tryout before signing that afternoon and then playing on Sunday.

The draft looked good on paper, as they took a hard-hitting safety Calvin Pryor out of Louisville in the first round. Drafting for need in the second round, they took Jace Amaro, a tight end from Texas Tech, and in the third they took Dexter McDougle, a cornerback out of Maryland. Making the transition from college football to the style of football played in the NFL is hard. As evidence of the how that draft didn't work out, those players should be the foundation of today's Jets, but only one of those 12 draft choices is still with the Jets today, and that's Quincy Enunwa, and he's struggled with injuries of late.

Ryan was doing his best to make the team competitive, but it wasn't working. They won the season opener against the Oakland Raiders 19–14 and then went on to lose eight straight games. I think it had more to do with the lack of talent rather than the lack of ability to coach.

The season ended with the Jets at the bottom of the AFC East with a 4–12 record. Ryan was fired and so was general manager John Idzik. Once again, the search was on for a new front office, players had uncertain job security, and the fans had to endure another year of rebuilding the organization.

One of the interesting signings in 2014 came in the month of March when the Jets signed Michael Vick to a one-year contract and released Mark Sanchez the same day. Everyone was aware of the trouble that Vick had with the law in 2007 when he pleaded guilty to his involvement in a dogfighting ring. Vick paid for his involvement by spending

21 months in a federal prison and losing millions of dollars. I'm a dog lover. I've had dogs my entire life, and the crimes that Vick committed were almost unthinkable, but everyone deserves a second chance at life. I found Vick to be very remorseful and very humbled to have a second chance. Vick was coming to the Jets after playing five years with the Philadelphia Eagles, following his reinstatement into the NFL by Roger Goodell. Vick started three games for the Jets in 2014 and later ended his career with the Pittsburgh Steelers.

I remember getting into an argument with my ex-wife, Kelley, about Vick, telling her that everyone deserves a second chance because everyone makes mistakes. I explained that he paid dearly for his mistake with 21 months in prison, losing millions of dollars, and that he would be haunted the rest of his life for his involvement in those crimes. Wasn't that enough restitution? But she just wasn't buying any of it. She wanted him banned for life for what he did. That was her opinion, and I had mine.

When I met Vick in 2014, he was a changed man, a man on a mission, a man who was looking toward the future, and most importantly, a man who had paid for the sins he committed in the past.

Make no mistake: Vick's coach on the Jets—Ryan—was good for the Jets and he's good for the NFL. He's an excellent football coach. He knows his Xs and Os on the defensive side of the ball, but he also wanted the attention and spotlight that came with the job title. What I like about him was that you would meet him for the first time, have a conversation, and it was like talking to an old friend that you hadn't seen in years. What Ryan also did for the organization in his first two years was something special. He made two AFC Championship Game appearances.

But in the end, Ryan was probably his own worst enemy. In life it's important to be humble, thankful for the opportunities you have, and respectful of your opponents in victories or losses. From Day One Ryan came in stirring the pot when he said he wasn't kissing any rings and was going to take the Jets to the Super Bowl. Every press conference was must-see television with a *Saturday Night Live*-type of atmosphere. You never knew what Ryan was going to say or do. But the spotlight was always there for Ryan. From running with the bulls to foot fetish signs in New England, he was true to his own personality. Ryan was good for the Jets, but in the end the song got old, the dance floor was empty, and it was time to hire a new band.

It was a never-ending, roller-coaster ride for the Jets. Hold on tight. Here we go again. They had to search for both a new head coach and a new general manager. Also on the top of their grocery list was finding a quarterback and other skill players. You can improve a team through free agency, but you must build a team through the draft. That would be the challenge for the Jets ownership in the 2015 offseason. They had to develop stability at the top first and then work their way down to the locker room. The biggest question was whether they would be looking for a new head coach with offensive knowledge or defensive knowledge. The game had changed from the style of football that was played when I was in the league when a great defensive team would beat a great offense. That really wasn't the case anymore. To win in today's NFL, you must score points. The next head coach had a big challenge in front of him, and whoever they hired had big shoes to fill when it came to be matching the personality of Ryan.

My house phone rang in the early hours on January 26, 2015. It was around 1:00 AM. My wife answered the call and suddenly dropped to her knees in tears, yelling Sean has died. Sean was our 17-year-old nephew. Like many kids his age, he was full of life and had so much to give this world. Sean had gone out with a group of friends on a snowy night to go tubing in the snow. He lost control of the tub and hit a light pole, ending his life. Sean was special. He could walk into a room, and the room would light up with laughter. He had a smile that was contagious.

For all of the holidays, the Lyons family was either at Sean's parents' house or ours. I watched Sean grow from a little boy to a star soccer player in high school, but he wasn't just a good athlete. He was a good kid. Like other families who lose a child, it changes your life forever. The void in your heart never repairs itself. Holidays aren't the same. Birthdays can't be celebrated the same way, even though we tell ourselves that tomorrow will be a little better than today.

I found myself asking why once again the good Lord would take someone with so much to offer this world. There are no answers that were acceptable, and once again death challenged my faith. Sean's wake was endless from the time the doors opened until the time they closed the funeral home. Everyone—young and old—had a story about Sean and everyone was still in disbelief. On the same day 37 years earlier, I lost the man, Coach Bryant, who molded me into the person I am today.

As a professional athlete, you sometimes think of yourself as a person who can handle everything thrown your way. As a football player, the game is simple: hit the guy in front of you and tackle the guy with the ball. The passion you play the game with is the same passion you need to play the game of life with. But the only thing we all have in common is death. One day we're all going to die.

I've gone to too many wakes and have done too many eulogies to think otherwise. When you lose a loved one, the world continues. Healing is an endless process. When someone that you care about dies, they leave a piece of themselves in every one of us, and it's our duty and our responsibility to keep them alive in our hearts.

These thoughts struck me when I got the tragic news that a former teammate of mine, Barry Bennett and his wife, Carol, were murdered in their home in Long Prairie, Minnesota, on August 23, 2019. Barry was a great teammate, a true Christian, and a guy who loved his family. His best friend was his wife, Carol. They did everything together. Barry did anything for anyone and never asked for anything in return. That's what made him so special. He never talked about his career in the NFL. He talked about how he could mold young students into good people by teaching them the values of life. Barry did that as a coach and a teacher at the local high school. Making it even harder to take was that their son, Dylan, was charged with the murder.

After getting the news, I found myself asking once again why. I've always believed that God has a plan for each one of us, but where does this crime fit into that plan? I do know that we must come together in our fight on gun control and mental health. It's time for all of us to stand up to the issues that affect our future.

* * *

The Jets hired Mike Maccagnan as their general manager and Todd Bowles as their new head coach. Both are good men. Maccagnan was on the quiet side, but he knew his football. Bowles came from the Arizona Cardinals, where he was the defensive coordinator. Both had the experience in the NFL, but for both it was their first time running an organization.

Their first task was to find a quarterback around whom to build the team. They settled on Ryan Fitzpatrick. They also brought back former players, Darrelle Revis and Antonio Cromartie, and traded for a talented wide receiver in Brandon Marshall. During the draft they upgraded their defensive line with Leonard Williams. The knock on Fitzpatrick in the NFL rumor mill was that he was a quality quarterback who was too inconsistent. He'd follow a good game or a good year with a bad game and a bad year. It was like riding a roller coaster. Fitzpatrick was a journeyman in the NFL. He spent time with the Buffalo Bills from 2009 to 2012. He got a big contract from the Bills in 2011 and then was released after the 2012 season. He went to the Tennessee Titans for a year, then to the Houston Texans for a year, and then he was the Jets' starting quarterback. His career numbers with the Bills were 80 touchdowns and 64 interceptions. In his previous 10 seasons in the NFL with five other teams, he had 123 touchdowns and 101 interceptions. That's a roller-coaster ride if you ever saw one.

Bowles was a quiet man who didn't show a great deal of emotion on the sidelines when things went south, but in private he challenged his players and kept important team matters in house. That works when you're winning, but if you're losing, you better know your players, and they better respect your authority.

The challenge for Bowles and his coaching staff was to improve on the 4–12 season from 2014 and to get the players to buy into his coaching philosophy. The Jets started off fast, going 4–1 in their first five games. It looked like it was going to be a magical season. Bowles came in after the game and allowed me to ask the first question in his press conference, but he never gave an opening statement on the game itself. He allowed me to open the floor with whatever I thought was important. One thing for sure: Bowles always took the bullet for his players in the press conference. He never once called out a player or threw one of them under the bus.

From Week Six to Week 10, the Jets found themselves in fight every week and went 1–4. So after 10 games, the Jets had cooled off with a 5–5 record with six games to go in the season. The Jets didn't start pointing fingers, which was a credit to Bowles. The NFL season is demanding and long, so you must grind it on, and that's what the Jets did by winning five in a row.

With a record of 10–5, the Jets faced a Bills team coached by Rex Ryan—yep, that Rex Ryan—on the road. Win and you're in, lose and the season would be over. Fitzpatrick was having a banner year with 29 touchdowns and 12 interceptions heading into the game. All he had to do was manage the game, protect the ball, and win against a 7–8 Bills team for the Jets to make it to the playoffs. It didn't happen. The Jets lost that game to Buffalo 22–17, and Fitzpatrick's stat line told the story. Fitzpatrick passed for 181 yards and two touchdowns, but he also threw three interceptions in the fourth quarter to seal the loss. Fitzpatrick had a career year, setting a franchise record with 31 passing touchdowns. The Jets seemed like they were moving in the right direction by going 10–6, but once again they would have to wait until next season to try to make the playoffs.

Lyons Life Lesson

Everyone is entitled to have an opinion and to voice their opinion. It doesn't mean your opinion is right or wrong. What it does mean is that's what you think and believe, and that's okay. To make this world better, we should be respectful of everyone's opinion even if it's different from our own.

Football will never define me, and don't let your career or what the outside world thinks about you define you. Define yourself with the passion of helping others and live life to its fullest every day. Ask yourself at the end of the day: did I make this world better today? If the answer is yes, that's great. Then do it again tomorrow. If the answer is no, then try harder tomorrow.

CHAPTER 22

Trying Times of 2016–18

Coming off a 10–6 season in 2015, even though the team didn't make it to the playoffs for the sixth consecutive year, the organization felt energized. Todd Bowles had the respect of the team, and it felt like things were moving in the right direction. One of the first moves they made in the offseason was signing Ryan Fitzpatrick to a one-year, fully guaranteed contract worth $12 million. Fitzpatrick had a great season in 2015 (except the final game against the Buffalo Bills) while throwing for 31 touchdowns and only 15 interceptions. But in the past, Fitzpatrick had followed a good year with a bad year.

You have to build for the future through the draft. That's the way to success in the NFL, so the Jets drafted Darron Lee, an outside linebacker out of Ohio State, in the first round. Not a lot of the other 31 teams had Lee ranked so high, but the Jets took him 20th overall. Maybe Lee had to develop and gain some weight, but the Jets had big plans for him to be an impact player. In the second round, they drafted who they felt would be the quarterback of the future for them in Christian Hackenberg out of Penn State. This was a reach for the Jets since no other NFL team had Hackenberg higher than a fifth-round pick. What did the Jets know that the other 31 NFL team didn't know?

The Jets preseason was uneventful and they went 1–3. In this day and age in the NFL, you really don't learn a lot about your team in preseason, and records are meaningless. The key is making it through the preseason healthy so you can start the regular season with a fresh start.

After going 1–1 in their first two games, the Jets had a disastrous performance in their third game of the season, which came against the Kansas City Chiefs. To win in the NFL, you normally must succeed in two of the three parts of the game: offense, defense, or special teams to have a puncher's chance of winning. The Jets lost two of three that afternoon, and that would define the 2016 season. On offense they had eight turnovers! Fitzpatrick threw six interceptions, and the team fumbled twice, including once on special teams. The Chiefs returned a fumble for a touchdown and returned one of the interceptions for a touchdown.

Midway through the third quarter, we got a knock on the radio booth door from Bobby Parente, telling Bob Wischusen and I to tone it down about the interceptions. If I remember correctly, we stated in a respectful way during our broadcast that maybe it was time to take Fitzpatrick out of the game and put in the backup quarterback. These comments didn't come until after he threw his fourth interception of the day. Parente was one of the vice presidents with the Jets and he would grab a headset and listen to our broadcast of away games. Parente was known for telling us to stay positive during tough times, and we always knew he had our back. Wischusen paints the pictures for our listeners. I try to analyze why the play worked or failed. Fitzpatrick was having a bad day. We weren't saying to bench him for the next game. We were just stating what we saw that day and what we felt was best for the team that day. Did we tone it down? I'm not sure if we did. I, though, am sure that Fitzpatrick threw six interceptions that day. The Jets offensive possessions chart read: 10 possessions, six interception, two punts, one field goal, and one fumble. An ugly chart like that will not win many games in the NFL. With all the mistakes the Jets made that afternoon in Kansas City, they only lost 24–3. The defense only allowed 10 points, but you win as team and you lose as a team.

That game in Kansas City defined Fitzpatrick for the entire season. He was benched twice that year for Geno Smith and Bryce Petty and ended up only starting 11 games for the Jets. His final stats for the year were 2,710 passing yards, 12 touchdowns, and 17 interceptions. That's how Fitzpatrick's resume read: good year and then a bad year. The Jets also had a bad year, taking a step back to finish the season with an 5–11 record and for the sixth consecutive year they didn't make it to the playoffs. They finally cut ties with Fitzpatrick after the season. They had the quarterback for the future waiting for his chance in Hackenberg, right?

The Jets struggled in 2016, so I took solace in my bowling outings with Jesse, one of the children helped by the foundation. (Marty Lyons Foundation)

The 2017 season began in January for the radio crew. We have a thing where we all have to lose all the weight we gained from the previous season. I think I gained about 25 pounds from the start to the end. I wasn't the biggest gainer that year, though, as Joe Loughran, the producer, must have gained more than 40 pounds. For me it was back to the gym and back to walking and watching what I ate. My goal was to lose all 25 by the start of training camp in July.

Coming off another disappointing season of 5–11, the Jets had to tighten things up as well. Changes were coming for the 2017 Jets, and that started early in February when they started shipping players out the door. Longtime center Nick Mangold was released in February. Besides being a pillar on the offensive line for years, he was a team leader and one of the players who represented the Jets in the community with class and respect. Mangold was fighting through injuries from the previous season, and the Jets were trying to get younger at his position. Darrelle

Revis, another class individual, was shown the door. Revis Island would take his talent to another NFL team and wait for his call from Canton, Ohio, where one day he'll be inducted into the NFL Hall of Fame. David Harris, a starting middle linebacker who did everything for the Jets since the day he was drafted out of the University of Michigan, was cut loose. Harris was the heart and soul of the defense, but nothing lasts forever. Other notable veterans who were given an apple and a road map were kicker Nick Folk, wide receiver Eric Decker, offensive lineman Breno Giacomini, and wide receiver Brandon Marshall.

The changing of the roster didn't stop there as the Jets started trading some of their past draft choices to other NFL teams. Former No. 1 draft picks Calvin Pryor and Sheldon Richardson were traded to the Cleveland Browns and Seattle Seahawks, respectively. I really liked Richardson. I tried to take him under my wing, but he started to drift away from being the outstanding player on the playing field to finding himself in bad off-the-field situations. In life every man must hold themselves accountable for their own actions, and the Jets had enough with Richardson.

The faces on the Jets were changing, and names on the back of the jerseys were different. The 2017 draft was one of the best drafts that I've seen in a long time as the Jets went to the SEC for their first three picks. They selected Jamal Adams out of LSU with the sixth overall pick in the first round, and the hard-hitting safety brings it every single play. Marcus Maye, another safety, was selected in the second round out of Florida, and in the third round, they went back to Alabama and selected wide receiver ArDarius Stewart. The Jets were building for the future with the hope that these three players could make a smooth transition from college football to the NFL.

A few weeks before training camp, I hosted my golf outing for the Marty Lyons Foundation on July 10 and sat on a par 3 for the entire day meeting and greeting the golfers. It was a hot day, but I felt great. I had gotten myself back in shape. For the first time in a long time, I was right where I wanted to be with my weight. I was under 260 pounds. I had all my kids and grandchildren at the event, and the dinner went great as we raised a lot of money for the foundation.

We returned home, had a bite to eat, and talked about how we were going to make all the airport runs the next day. Around 2:30 in the morning, both of my legs went into a full body cramp, waking me from a sound sleep. Not wanting to wake my wife, Christine, I rolled out of bed and tried to stand to relieve the cramps. That was the last thing I remember until I opened my eyes to find myself surrounded by my sons, Rocky and Jesse, who are both doctors. I had passed out. After they checked my blood pressure, which had gone through the roof, they called 911. I couldn't fight the fact that I passed out, and the next stop was the emergency room.

When I got to the emergency room, the doctors started doing their tests. Two of my closest friends, Dr. Brian McKenna and Dr. Ernie Vomero, showed up. I didn't realize that Jesse had reached out to them to let them know what had happened. It didn't take them long to bring me to the emergency room and make the decision to transfer me to another hospital where Dr. Vomero was more involved. Before I got transferred, I noticed that something had happened with my eyesight. I was seeing double.

Once I got to the second hospital, they started running tests, including MRIs, brain scans, and blood tests. They were pumping me with fluids through IVs to make sure I wasn't dehydrated. Around 7:30 AM I was going down the halls of the hospital for an MRI, and that's when I saw my former teammate Wesley Walker walk by. He was so kind and spread the word about my condition. I ended up spending two days in the hospital, and my eyesight seemed to correct itself.

After being discharged from the hospital, I went home and took a nap but woke up with double vision again. I went back for another MRI, and they found the problem. I suffered a mild stroke, which caused a

Josh McCown impressed me with his leadership during a rough 2017 season. (New York Jets)

cranial nerve IV palsy. That means that a certain muscle in your eye is paralyzed. Dr. Vomero got the wheels in motion with an appointment with an neurologist named Dr. Patrick Sibony. He was the best in his field and also happened to be on Long Island.

Dr. Sibony was honest as he sat with Christine, Jesse, and me. He reassured me that my eyesight would heal itself over time. After reading the MRI, he told me that this was the second stroke that I had. The first one scarred my brain but didn't affect me physically. God was watching over me.

Do you believe that God sends us signs from above to help us deal with our health problems? Our foundation had a young girl named Katie who had cancer. Katie's dream vacation was a trip to Walt Disney World for her and her family. Before she left for the trip, she was out with her father shopping when she saw a machine that had an egg-like shape objects in it with a prize in each one. She entered some quarters, and when the egg-like object came down, Katie opened it and found a special coin. It was a two-headed coin that had an angel on both sides. Katie showed the coin to her father saying, "One day I'm going to be an angel and I'll be able to fly."

After Katie got back from her trip to Disney World, she was admitted into the hospital and took a turn for the worse. They moved her to the ICU, and I met them at the hospital. Once we got to Katie's room, we gathered around the bed and joined hands. I asked God to please take care of Katie. I left that afternoon, knowing that Katie's future was in God's hands, not ours. When my phone rang on Wednesday just three days later, I didn't have to answer it. I knew by the caller ID number that Katie had earned her wings. She was an angel. That double-sided coin gave peace and comfort to Katie. She believed it was a sign from God, and so do I.

My health issues could not compare to what poor Katie suffered through. But for the first time in my life I got to experience what it was like to be handicapped. It was also the first time I missed a radio broadcast. As it worked out, I missed the entire preseason.

As I sat at home and listened to the Jets radio during my recovery, my partner, Wischusen, gave the listeners an update on my health and when I would possibly return to the booth. After the third game, Jesse said, "Boy, Dad, Bob really loves you. Maybe you should have him do your eulogy if something happens." I reminded Jesse that I wasn't going anywhere anytime soon, but I would take that under consideration.

I can't tell you when my eyes started to heal themselves, but I can tell you I got more letters and phone calls with more thoughts and prayers than you can imagine. Christine tore into my backside one day. She said, "Stop feeling sorry for yourself," and that was the same day that I went for my checkup. As we sat in the waiting room, I watched all the other patients come in. Some came in using walkers, some came in using wheelchairs, and some came in with facial displacements. After I got examined, I told Christine that if this was God's plan for me the rest of my life that I was okay with it. From that day on, my prayers at night were simple. I just asked the good Lord to make my eyes a little better tomorrow than it was today. I returned to work wearing an eye patch and set my sights on being with the Jets as they opened the 2017 season in Buffalo against the Bills.

Josh McCown was the only bright spot for the 2017 New York Jets. McCown was known throughout the league as a journeyman because he played for 10 teams since he was drafted in 2002 in the third round by the Arizona Cardinals. People say that certain people are born to be leaders. I believe people develop into leaders by the supporting cast around them. But either way McCown was a leader. The Jets brought him into training camp to work with their two young quarterbacks, Hackenberg and Petty. What the Jets didn't expect was McCown was going to win the starting job. He started 13 games in 2017, throwing for almost 3,000 yards and 18 touchdowns and only nine interceptions. He won both the Curtis Martin MVP award and the Kyle Clifton award, which is awarded to a "good guy" on the team. Teammates are the ones who vote for both of these distinguished awards. McCown was a true professional. He played hard, and his leadership was always positive. The Jets had a diamond in the rough. If they could draft a quarterback in the 2018 draft, they knew they had a mentor, a player/coach who could mold that player into a franchise quarterback.

I met another person who could inspire. Rosemary was a bubbly teenager with a bright future when cancer entered her body. She was loved by all, especially her mother and grandmother, and they were by her side every day during her fight. Whenever I had a bad day, I would get in my car and I'd go visit the kids in the hospital. It was my way of coming back to reality of what really was important. On one bad day when I was yelling and cursing, I decided I would go over unannounced and surprise Rosemary with a visit. When I got to her room, she was sleeping. The chemotherapy had beaten up her body. She had lost her hair, the brightness of her skin had faded, her stomach was swollen, and dark circles had settled in under her eyes. I stood at the door for almost 15 minutes looking at Rosemary, knowing that cancer was winning this battle. Out of nowhere Rosemary opened her eyes. They still had a sparkle. The first words out of her mouth were "my wig." She didn't want me to see her without her wig. Before Rosemary started her treatment, she had long black hair below her shoulders. That afternoon we laughed together like there was no tomorrow. We talked about faith and family and in our hearts we knew that this would be the last time we would share life together. Rosemary was another gift from God, who was taken away way too early from us.

* * *

After going 5–11 the year before, Todd Bowles was entering his fourth year as the head coach of the New York Jets. He wasn't just on a slippery rope. He was on slippery ice, not just because of his win-loss record, but also the team was changing. Life in the NFL changes every year. You have new faces, old faces, and missing faces. Nobody said coaching in the NFL was easy, especially with free agency in play.

The Jets moved up in the draft to get their franchise quarterback, Sam Darnold out of USC, with the third overall pick. Darnold had all the tools: a strong arm, good feet, a high football IQ, and had a good head on his shoulders. Just maybe Darnold would be the answer to all for the longtime suffering Jets fans and change the direction the organization. He would need to perform not only for his teammates and the fans, but also for Bowles to keep his job.

The Jets opened their season on the road against a Detroit Lions team that was rebuilding themselves. On the first play, Darnold threw a pick-six, and within seconds the franchise quarterback had put his team in a 7–0 hole. But you don't judge a player by one play. You judge a player by his body of work.

Darnold rebounded from his terrible first play to guide the Jets to a 48–17 victory, completing 16 of his 21 passing attempts while throwing for two touchdowns. Break out the Kool-Aid, boys and girls. The Jets had their franchise quarterback. Or did they? It was just one game. But everyone felt good about the direction of the team with the Miami Dolphins coming up in Week Two. The Jets came out flat and lost 20–12, but most thought that was okay because we were playing the Cleveland Browns who had lost 19 straight games.

The Jets came out on fire and jumped out to an early lead. Then right before halftime, they changed quarterbacks and brought in the No. 1 draft pick from the 2018 draft, quarterback Baker Mayfield who was also the Heisman Trophy winner from the previous year, and the stadium came alive. Mayfield excited the fans and brought the Browns back to win the game 20–12. With that loss the Jets fell to 1–2, and everyone started to forget about the Detroit game. Instead people started to feel these were the same old Jets.

The losses kept coming that year, and the Jets finished 4–12 and in last place in the AFC East. The rope got too slippery for Bowles to hold onto, and he was fired at the end of the season. What really bothered me was the way some of the players approached the game. What happened to accountability? Players weren't showing up for meetings. They were late for practice. Some might point at the coach for the lack of discipline or losing the team. I leaned more toward players not holding themselves accountable. Players need to know what a privilege it is to play in the NFL. Players need to realize it's not the name on back of the jersey that matters. It's the name on the front. I really liked Bowles, but to coach here in New York, you must show your emotions. But that wasn't his personality, and with the team not performing, it was time to let him go.

Remember there are only two types of coaches in the NFL: those who have been fired and those who will be fired.

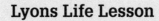

Lyons Life Lesson

You never know how much you should show appreciation for something or someone until they are taken away from you. Cherish every moment you have with loved ones and respect the gifts that you are blessed with.

CHAPTER 23
The 2019 Season

After Todd Bowles was fired and with the Jets having a lot of money to spend in free agency, change did happen. Everyone thought the other shoe was going to fall and that the team would fire general manager Mike Maccagnan, but that didn't happen—at least initially. The Jets allowed Maccagnan to spend money on free agents, prepare for the draft, and lead the way to finding their next new head coach. From the outside looking in, many thought a fresh start meant that the Jets were going to totally rebuild with a new head coach and a new general manager, but for now Maccagnan had some job security and some power.

The Jets were on their way to changing their culture—not only on the field, but also at their Florham Park, New Jersey, complex. They got new uniforms and added a new logo for the first time since 1998. The Jets made their first big move on January 1 when they hired Adam Gase, the former Miami Dolphins head coach as their new head coach. This was the first time I could remember them hiring an offensive-minded coach. Gase came to the Jets after spending three years with the Dolphins, where he took them to the playoffs in his first season. Since the Jets hadn't been to the playoffs since 2010, it was a breath of fresh air to get a new head coach that could work and communicate with their young quarterback, Sam Darnold.

The Jets made the headlines when they landed one of the most talented, gifted athletes in the NFL when they picked up Le'Veon Bell. He was going to be that running back carrying the ball 20 to 25 times a game, catching seven to 10 passes a game. Yes, indeed this was a home run. They also got a possession receiver in Jamison Crowder to help the offense and an offensive lineman, Kelechi Osemele. Maccagnan didn't forget about the defense either. He went out and got a Pro Bowl middle linebacker in C.J. Mosley from the Baltimore Ravens. With those pieces added, the rest of the Jets could be added through the draft.

With their first-round pick, the Jets took defensive tackle Quinnen Williams out of Alabama. Williams was an All-American with great size, good speed, and a high football IQ. Plus, he came from my alma mater of Alabama, which was another bonus for me. They drafted Jachai Polite, a linebacker out of the University of Florida; an offensive lineman, Chuma Edoga, out of USC; Trevon Wesco, a tight end out of West Virginia; and a linebacker out of Minnesota in Blake Cashman. Overall, Maccagnan and his scouts seemed to have successfully bolstered both sides of the ball.

On May 15 the other shoe fell dropped, as the Jets fired Maccagnan and appointed Gase as the interim general manager. Wait, let's go through that again. *The Jets kept Maccagnan on during free agency and the draft and then fired him?* Yep, that's what happened. Now the search to hire a new general manager was going to be led by owner Chris Johnson, Gase, and Hymie Elhai. The search for a new general manager would be key to changing the culture of the Jets, a process that was long overdue at 1 Jets Drive.

On June 7 Johnson and his committee hired Joe Douglas, who had all the experience you would look for in an individual in being a leader, as the new GM. He was a football guy, having spent 14 years with the Ravens working under and for Ozzie Newsome. To me, that was enough to tell me that they hired the right guy. I played with Newsome in college at Alabama, respected him as a player, respected him as an executive in the NFL, and loved him as a friend. Also, Douglas had a history with Gase. The two worked together in Chicago. On paper this was a perfect fit. Douglas was a former offensive lineman in his playing days at the University of Richmond who knew something about building a team. With three Super Bowl rings, Douglas had the vision that could change the Jets for years to come.

One of the first things that happened after Douglas was hired was that he started to bring the business side of the Jets together with the football side. With that in mind, tough changes had to be made. Elhai became the new president of the Jets, Brian Friedman became the new executive vice president and new chief operating officer, and Eric Gelfand became the senior vice president of communications and content. You could feel the energy in the building coming together, but would that translate into more wins in the 2019 season? Would that energy be enough to take the team to the playoffs, a place they hadn't been since 2010?

One of Gase's first hires was defensive coordinator Gregg Williams, a move that I loved. He was old school and reminded me of Walt Michaels. Williams believed in working hard and playing hard, and no one was more important than the guy next to you. He emphasized trusting your gameplan and your teammates. He would be an asset for the success of the Jets in the upcoming season.

Gase ran a very disciplined training camp. Players moved from one spot to another, running not walking. Players, who couldn't practice because of injuries, rode bikes. Changes were made, and the results would be on the football field not in preseason games, which in my opinion are a joke. Players aren't playing because the teams are trying to protect them from injuries. Don't get me wrong: new players need to play, but building chemistry is so important as you get ready for a season. The biggest thing that came out the 2019 preseason was the loss of Avery Williamson, a key member of the Jets defense. Williamson had an outstanding year in 2018, was a veteran player, and a great locker room guy.

Opening day for the Jets came against the Buffalo Bills, an AFC East opponent, on September 8 at home in MetLife Stadium. It was the start of a new era with Douglas and Gase running the show, but don't forget this 2019 team was put together by Maccagnan. He was responsible for the draft and the players the Jets got during free agency.

The stadium was rocking on Opening Day. The fans were excited to see their new Jets and the new uniforms. Bob Wischusen and I were starting our 18th season calling the games on radio. I've seen the good, the bad, and the ugly over my 41 years of being in the Jets family. And yes, I was also a part of the good, the bad, and the ugly as a player, but this year felt different. Maybe it was just the fact the whole organization seemed to be on the same page.

The Jets had complete control of the game against the Bills for the first 45 minutes and took a 16-point lead into the fourth quarter. Now it was time to time to put the game away—except quarterback Josh Allen and the Bills still had fight left in them. The Jets let the Bills back in the game and lost by one point in the closing minute. That happens in the NFL. Sometime a young team doesn't know how to close a team out. I could accept that it would be a lesson that they would have to learn. But the biggest loss for the Jets that day wasn't the final score. It was losing Mosley with a pulled groin. He was one of the big signings during free agency and a player who led by example—not by talking. Losing both of your starting linebackers would hurt the Jets, but if Coach Williams was as good as people thought he was, he'd find a way to have the next-man-up theory play out. Williams could build a player up to play better than his talent level. He also could break a player down very quickly by benching him for blowing an assignment during a game. He would have to balance that coaching quality over the course of the 2019 season.

The time in between games goes by quickly in the NFL, and the Jets next had a big *Monday Night Football* game against the Cleveland Browns and their young quarterback, Baker Mayfield, making for a matchup of two promising quarterbacks in Darnold and Mayfield. But early in the week, Darnold came down with mono and would miss the next three games because of his illness. The Jets went out before the season and got a veteran backup quarterback in Trevor Siemian just in case something happened to Darnold, but this was only Week Two. Siemian didn't last too long as he was knocked out of the game with an ankle injury after throwing just six passes. In the NFL it's always next man up, which meant that the Jets had to go to their third-string quarterback, Luke Falk, who was just brought up from the Jets practice squad as a backup to Siemian until Darnold got healthy. The injury-depleted Jets fell to 0–2 after losing to the Browns 23–3.

Injuries are part of the game, and nobody, I mean nobody, was going to feel sorry for them, especially the New England Patriots, who they were playing in Week Three. Falk was driving the bus as the Jets dropped to 0–3 while falling 30–14. Starting fast in the NFL is a must, but it didn't seem like that was going to happen as the Jets entered an early bye week in Week Four of their schedule, hoping that Darnold would be back for their matchup with the Philadelphia Eagles, Douglas' old team and the winner of the Super Bowl in 2018. What would the Jets do? Well, Darnold didn't make it back, Falk tried his best, and the Jets dropped to a 0–4, losing to the Eagles 31–6.

With each loss the Jets dug themselves a deeper hole. Heat was turned up on Gase, the media was relentless about the team in a negative way, and the noise outside the Jets complex got louder and louder about Gase's hiring. It's hard enough to win the NFL with your starting quarterback, but how were you going to win with a quarterback who went from the practice squad to a starter in one week? You're on the practice squad for a reason, and it's to possibly develop into a player. Was it Gase's coaching that led to Darnold getting sick? No. Was it Gase's coaching that got Siemian hurt? No. But the finger always points to the head coach in the NFL, even though most of these players were not the choice of Gase nor Douglas. Bill Parcells once said, "If you want me to be the cook, let me choose the groceries."

With the Jets at 0–4, everyone was curious whether Gase could keep his team together. I knew some of the players in the locker room, and they believed in Gase, but if they didn't turn this thing around, the outside noise might get too loud for anyone to stand. At 0–4 the Jets just kept working, the locker room kept quiet, and they were getting ready for a possible return of Darnold and a Week Six matchup with America's Team, the Dallas Cowboys.

A little thinner and maybe still a little weak from his four-week battle with mono, Darnold was back as the Jets quarterback. The excitement of having him back and also playing the Cowboys made everyone seem to forget that the Jets were 0–4. By halftime the Jets had the fans on their feet. They were winning 21–6, and even the press box was buzzing that the Jets didn't look anything like what they had seen the last three weeks. *Duh, you have your starting quarterback back!* The only other guy that touches the ball the same amount of times in the game is the center. The Jets had a 21–9 lead, heading into the fourth quarter and they had learned about putting teams away after allowing Buffalo to come back and win in Week One. The Jets didn't play their best 15 minutes but earned their first win of the 2019 season after they beat the Cowboys 24–22. This was the start of climbing back in the game and back in the chase of the AFC East race. Or was it? If it was, the Jets could make a splash the following week on *Monday Night Football* against the Patriots, a team that beat them 30–14 in Week Three, but that was with Falk, not Darnold.

Nothing went right that night for the Jets. Darnold took a step back, made some poor decisions, didn't get any help from the defense, and the Jets fell to 1–5. Watching Darnold play that night, I could tell that he hadn't fully recovered from his mono. One, though, must give credit to Bill Belichick. He threw the kitchen sink at Darnold, blitzing from everywhere. That night the Jets got knocked down, but the key to becoming a champion is getting back up. With the Jets sliding to 1–5, maybe what they needed was to travel to Florida for back-to-back games against Jacksonville and Miami. If they could win both of those games, they would be 3–5 at the halfway point of the season.

At 1–5 and with the season starting to slip away, the injury bug hit the Jets once again. The key position in the NFL is the offensive line, and they were getting banged up. The Jets found themselves starting five different linemen almost every week and they were only approaching Week Eight.

The Jacksonville Jaguars aren't one of the powerhouse team in the NFL. They were 4–3, had lost their starting quarterback Nick Foles earlier in the season, and were starting a rookie quarterback named Gardner Minshew. His name was Gardner Flint Minshew II, to be exact. Minshew was a sixth-round pick in the 2019 draft out of Washington State and he could spin the ball. Minshew was a larger-than-life character for the Jaguars fans. He sported a 1970s mustache and dressed in a retro way. But make no mistake about it: Minshew was a good quarterback who was successful at every level that he played, including East Carolina, where he set all kinds of records.

The banged up Jets traveled to Jacksonville to play the 1–5 Jaguars and hoped for a win. But in the NFL, you can't hope for win. You must earn it. After matching touchdowns in the first quarter, things went south for the Jets. Bad decisions by Darnold and an unbalanced gameplan on the offensive side of the ball (the Jets only tried to run the ball 14 times for a total of 46 yards) cost them. Their big free-agent signing, Bell, had only eight rushing attempts for 23 yards, and Darnold struggled, ending the game, going 21-of-30 for 218 yards, two touchdowns, and three interceptions. The defense also allowed Jacksonville to rush for 111 yards while the rock star for the '70s, Minshew, threw for 279 yards and three touchdowns.

Now the Jets were in a free fall at 1–6. Players were getting hurt, being put on injured reserve, and getting moved from the practice squad to the starting lineup. And media was turning up the heat on Gase. What people don't realize is that you can only coach the talent that you have.

The next stop was against Gase's old team, the Dolphins, who were winless at 0–7. The focus all week in the media was about Gase playing his old team—not so much the Jets playing the Dolphins. When you play a winless team, everyone expects you to win without any effort. What people forget is that other team is also getting paid to win. What you really had was two teams desperate for a win since the Jets were 1–6 and the Dolphins were 0–7.

Though Sam Darnold got mono and struggled through the early part of the season, I think the quarterback still has a bright future. (New York Jets)

The Jets had the only score after the first quarter, scoring on a touchdown drive to take a 7–0 lead into the second quarter. But in that second quarter, the Jets scored five points, and the Dolphins put up three touchdowns, making the score at halftime 21–12. The biggest problem was the Jets' run defense. They were allowing Dolphins quarterback Ryan Fitzpatrick too many running lanes. Even at his age, he had no fear of tucking the ball and running with it. The crowd at Hard Rock Stadium was packed with Jets fans. Some had made the trip south for the game, and others were transplants living a life of retirement in the southern part of Florida. Growing in frustration, the Jets fans let the team have it as they headed to the locker room. They yelled at players, coaches, and, of course, Gase.

This game came down to the fourth quarter, and the Jets trailed 24–15. But the Jets had too many lost opportunities and too many turnovers. And once again that put the Jets on the backside of a loss to a winless team. New York lost 26–18. The media wasted no time criticizing everything Gase did. But the blame should have been a blanket approach, extending to everyone.

When you're 1–7 at the halfway point of the season, the backside of the season would tell you more about Gase than the front side of the season. Could he hold the team together? Could Gase keep the locker room together? Hell, could they win another game? No one feels sorry for teams in the NFL that were struggling, and next up for the Jets were the New York Giants who had problems of their own. The 2–7 Giants were losers of five straight and had a rookie quarterback in Daniel Jones.

What would happen after the first half of the season proved that Gase could coach. The Jets won their next three games against the Giants, Washington Redskins, and Oakland Raiders to bring their record to 4–7 with a trip to Cincinnati next on the schedule. The Bengals were going through a horrendous year. Going into Week 13 of the season, they were the only winless team in the NFL. *Certainly, the Jets wouldn't stub their toe and lose to the Bengals.* Well, that's exactly what they did. Poor execution, turnovers, sacks, and just not being ready to play dropped them to a 4–8 record. The Jets were officially knocked out of the playoffs with four games left.

Playing for your job in 2020 meant a lot and playing with pride meant even more. The Jets went on to beat the Dolphins at home the following week, improving their record to 5–8 before traveling to Baltimore for a *Thursday Night Football* game versus the red hot Ravens. No matter what the final score indicated in the 42–21 loss, the Jets were respectable in their game against the Ravens. But it dropped their record to 5–9 with two games left. Wins against the Pittsburgh Steelers and Bills left the Jets with a 7–9 record—certainly not what anyone expected.

When you do a debriefing about an event or season, you start with what went well and then you finish with what went wrong. First, this team had every reason to quit on the organization, their teammates, and the coaching staff, but they didn't. They had to develop young players in the face of adversity when they lost starters at almost every position. The coaching staff, starting with Gase, did their best coaching when the team didn't have anything to play for. Young players like safety Jamal Adams had a unbelievable year. He won his second straight Curtis Martin MVP award.

The Jets are moving in the right direction. Gase and Douglas have the pulse of this team. They have the pulse of New York, and their expectations of this team is at an all-time high.

Lyons Life Lesson

The day before the Ravens game, my phone rang at 6:05 AM. I've always believed that football doesn't define an individual, that life changes minute to minute, and nothing in life is guaranteed.

It was my brother, Richard, calling to tell me that my younger brother, Phil, had passed away in the early hours on December 11. All indications pointed to a massive heart attack. Phil was the youngest of seven children. He was 57 years old and the only sibling not to outlive my father, who died at the age of 58. Phil was a good soul. He helped everyone, loved everyone, and cared more about other people enjoying his hard work then he did himself.

My parents always believed that their children would reflect their values. Phil was the paint on the canvas. He wasn't perfect, but he was a pillar in his community, a great father and husband, and a friend to all. After I got off the phone, I started to reflect on death. Death will one day happen to all of us. I started thinking about faith. Faith is believing in something you can't see. And in death—if you have enough faith— you will be rewarded in seeing everything that you believed in. I knew right then that Phil was in heaven with God and reunited with love ones that had left us earlier in life: his wife, Sharon; our mom and dad; Aunt Irene; Uncle Len; his cousin, Little Lenny; and his nephew, Christopher. I wasn't sitting there asking the good Lord why. I accepted the fact the Phil was at his final resting place. It took away most of the pain, knowing where we all want to be one day—in heaven. Phil was just there a little sooner than anyone of us expected. As people read his eulogy, I realized the impact that he had in life. Rest in peace, Phil, enjoy heaven. They say that tears are a sign of strength, not weakness. If that is true, we all became a lot stronger through death.

Remember: define who you are by the way you live your life. The joy of life is seeing how others benefit from the way you live your life. Live, love, laugh, and be happy.

ACKNOWLEDGMENTS

Where do I start? If I start with names, I'm sure I will forget someone. Thank you to my lifelong friend, Lou Sahadi, for his support in helping me write this book. Thank you to my family and friends for always being there for me. My wife, Christine, for being the backbone of our family. My children, Rocky, Jesse, Megan, and Lucas, you make me proud for the individuals who you've become. Now make yourselves proud as you continue your journey in life. Thank you to all my teammates from high school, college, and the New York Jets. Thank you to the New York Jets organization for Leon Hess, Woody Johnson, and Chris Johnson for always believing in me and supporting the Marty Lyons Foundation. Thank you to my extended family at the foundation and all of children who have come through our doors. To the ones who survived, thank you for showing me what strength and courage really are. To those who left us way too early in life, thank you for your impact, and I hope that this book brings meaning to your lives.

To my extended family of teammates, coaches, and friends, thank you for believing in me. To my foundation staff and volunteers past and present, thank you for opening your hearts to the mission of the foundation. And most of all thank you to all the children and families of the Marty Lyons Foundation. We shared a lot of laughter and we cried a lot of tears, but your memories will never be forgotten. To everyone who shared in my journey, thank you for allowing me into your lives. To my father Leo and a young man named Keith, you touched my life in such a way that enabled me to write this book. Hopefully, I'll see you on the other side one day. Love to all.

Mike Altieri, a special thank you for your friendship, love, and support for the last 41 years. We cried together and we laughed together. You're Uncle Mike to my children and you're King Salami to my friends. You're the best.

And an MVP award to articulate editor Jeff Fedotin who dotted every i and crossed every t.

And lastly, I thank God for the path He gave me in life. It wasn't easy. There were plenty of mistakes made along the way, but in the end, I hope that my impact was heard and made a difference in others.

Remember to define who you are by the way you live your life. The joy of life is seeing how others benefit from the way you live your life.